WHAT PARENTS ARE SAYING

Having struggled with my child's addiction, Patty has become a source of hope and inspiration for me to work on my own recovery. Her fresh perspective has been invaluable for me and my work to heal from the impact of this disease. This book comes from her heart and desire to help parents and the loved ones of addicts to work on their own recovery. My hope is that this book will lead you onto your path as well.

Barbara S. Recovery Mom

One thing that I've learned as a father of a teen who struggles with addiction is the importance of practicing self-care. All of the information that I could find during these tough, emotional times were geared toward the addiction and my child. What about me?? Having a guide to help me take care of myself is priceless. This book is incredible in teaching me that when I'm better, my child strives to be better and the cycle breaks. It is a must read for any parent who is living in this nightmare. This book is the gift that I will give every friend who is struggling the way that my family and I have.

Jim C. Recovery Dad

Parenting a child with substance use disorder has the potential to overtake your life, whether your child is in active use, in treatment, or struggling with sobriety, or succeeding with their sobriety. Before I read this book, I didn't understand what it meant to have my own recovery journey. This book, with its refreshing candor and practical tips, provides the guidance I need to gain a sense of peace and stability in my life.

Adapting a new mindset and using the skills I've learned from this book has been transformational for me, not just in my relationship with my son, but also with others in my family and at my job.

Sam G. Recovery Mom

How To Survive Your Child's Addiction

How To Survive Your Child's Addiction

A GUIDE TO RECOVERING PEACE AND REDISCOVERING JOY

Patty Stanek Fallone

Published by Best Seller Publishing®, St. Augustine, FL
Best Seller Publishing® is a registered trademark.
Printed in the United States of America.
ISBN: 978-1-959840-98-5

This publication is designed to provide accurate and authoritative information with regard to the subject matter covered. It is sold with the understanding that the publisher is not engaged in rendering legal, accounting, or other professional advice. If legal advice or other expert assistance is required, the services of a competent professional should be sought. The opinions expressed by the author in this book are not endorsed by Best Seller Publishing® and are the sole responsibility of the author rendering the opinion.

For more information, please write:
Best Seller Publishing®
53 Marine Street
St. Augustine, FL 32084
or call 1 (626) 765-9750
Visit us online at: www.BestSellerPublishing.org

Disclaimer

The examples of situations in this book are compilations of stories that have been shared with me over the years. The have been fictionalized for privacy purposes. Any resemblance to real people and real situations is to be expected. The difficult situations we face as parents of addicts are predictable and common. We all face the similar problems with different details. Except for my own stories, none of the stories divulge details of anyone else's personal story.

Cover art by Marian Stahl Chamberlain - marianstahlchamerblain.com

EPIGRAPH

*Sometimes you can only find heaven by
slowly backing away from hell.*

CARRIE FISHER

*Hope is being able to see the light
despite all of the darkness.*

DESMOND TUTU

CONTENTS

DEDICATION

This book is dedicated, with love, to all those who struggle because their loved one struggles, those who hurt because their loved one is in pain, and those who have lost themselves along the way, trying to do the impossible and fix them. I get it. I've been there.

You can stop and breathe now. You have permission to do what you need to do to be okay. You have permission to walk away from shame and guilt to create a better life for yourself. You did not cause this. You may not have been perfect, but you did your best. Know that in every word here, there is love and there is an offer of hope for you, a hope that you find a path to recovering peace and to rediscovering joy in your life no matter what challenges you are facing. You deserve it. You've earned it. It's waiting for you. You have the power, I promise.

ACKNOWLEDGEMENTS

Thank you, my son Patrick, for getting sober. Thank you for knowing that you were meant for more. Thank you Katie, Yaya, and Anthony for forgiving me for being consumed by Patrick. Thank you all for allowing the healing to take place in our family and for being a constant source of joy and pride for me. And to my children and their partners, thank you for being so supportive as I tell my version of our stories. Thank you for allowing me to drone on about the book process and for all of your insights and valued opinions both on the book and everything else in life. You have given me the life I dreamed of.

Thank you to Barbara who has been with me every step of the way with this book providing honest feedback, a sounding board, and the sagest advice I could hope for. Thank you also to Jim, Sam, Donna, Mary, Fred, and Heather who have humored my neediness through the process and encouraged me along the way. Thank you to Alexandra Deubner, my coach, thank you for telling me I could actually write a book. To Sara Connell and my TLA sisters—thank you for getting me to actually write the book.

And finally, for all the people who helped me on my own journey of recovery, that lead to this book; Ben Steefle with Caron in PA, Lauren Springer, Diana Clarke and Tom Marzilli with

Turnbridge in CT, and all my Al-Anon and recovery friends and sponsors. I hope this book provides for others the wisdom that you have bestowed on me.

INTRODUCTION

On September 11, 2016, I walked into the chapel service at the Caron Treatment Center in Pennsylvania. I had sent my kids in ahead of me while I took a couple of deep breaths, fighting back the tears I no longer had the strength to cry. I pulled back my hunched and heavy shoulders and went in feeling like I was entering into a different dimension. Time had stopped for me by that point. My life had become laser-focused on trying to fix the mess that my son's life had become.

I have always found comfort in sacred spaces, and as emotional as this moment was, and despite all the pain and confusion that had brought me here, there was a peace and an energy that was, not shockingly, very comforting. The Chit Chat Auditorium, at Caron, is a large space. It seats about two hundred, with large windows surrounding the altar space, framing the glaring overcast skies beyond them on that day. I stood in the back, as I often do in situations like this, refusing the seat I had been offered so I could scan the room and take it all in. I do this mostly because, at a mere five feet, I usually can't see anything if I sit. What I saw was people, lots of people—young, old, clients, families, staff. I looked around and had one overpowering thought. *These are my new peeps. I am the mother of a drug addict. How the hell did this happen?*

That particular Sunday happened to be the fifteenth anniversary of my husband Anthony's death on 9/11, in the Twin

Towers, on the 105th floor of the North Tower. It had been his seventh week at Cantor Fitzgerald. My son Patrick, who was to have had his first full day of kindergarten way back then, now a nineteen-year-old addict, about three weeks sober and two weeks into the Caron Young Men's program, had been assigned a task for chapel. He was to write and share a goodbye letter to his father. More deep breaths for me. Two of my other three children and I were in Pennsylvania for a family education weekend program. We saw Patrick earlier in the morning, and he informed us that he had written the letter and had shared it with his group, but, although he would speak, he would not be reading the letter at chapel. Thank God for small favors because I didn't know how I would make it through that. During the chapel service, he spoke, addressing the attentive audience, then I spoke after him, though I really don't remember much of what either of us said.

After speaking, I returned to my spot in the back corner and listened to other clients and family members share about their struggles with addiction and the hope they now had when a large group stood up and surrounded the altar. I thought, *wow, what a supportive family, they brought everybody!* When I realized what was happening it was like a battering ram to my gut. The shaking parents held the ashes of their twenty-four-year-old son, who had overdosed and was found dead in his car a considerable time later. That's when it really hit me. My kids and I weren't on this weekend just to learn about addiction and understand Patrick. We were there to learn how to be okay, whether Patrick was or not. There was still the very real possibility that he might never be okay. My precious youngest could end up in an urn being held by a crumbled me, surrounded by my crushed children. Still, there these devastated parents stood, surrounded by family, crushed but able to be grateful. Grateful for what Caron had offered them and their son, grateful that he was no longer suffering, heartbroken but still able to offer hope to the rest of us; hope that even if it doesn't go the way we pray it will, we can go on with peace.

My purpose in writing this book and sharing my story and the stories of many others I've heard over the years is to do as those parents did for me: offer you hope. But even more than hope, this book can serve as an empowerment guide to help you step out of the mental chaos that a child's addiction and mental health issues can cause and guide you back to a place where you, once again, have power in your own life. My intention is that this book helps you develop the tools to stop allowing your child's illness to run your life. Parents often find themselves in a position where their sick child calls all the shots. That doesn't help anyone. Using the tools in this book might not result in your child getting better. It can result in you getting better, and the healthier we are, the better we learn to show up for ourselves, the better we can show up for everyone in our lives. When we stop contributing to our loved ones' behaviors, when we allow them to feel the consequences of the messes they create themselves, sometimes it results in them getting help; sometimes it doesn't, but what it does do is it allows us to not be swallowed up by their disease along with them.

Seven years ago, if I had been given a choice between my son having cancer or being an addict, I would have chosen cancer, hands down. I grew up in a house where my mother's biggest fear was that one of us would use drugs. My siblings were raised in the '60s when guys were constantly shooting up in the schoolyard. I came along years later and it wasn't as visible to me, but to my mother, it was a constant threat. I remember yellowed and tattered newspaper articles slightly visible behind fresher ones tacked to my fridge with plastic magnets of states we had visited. My mother clipped every article about drugs for the fridge, an ode to what not to become. I knew what a stoner was from my own circles of friends, but I had no idea what drug use really looked like.

When my son started exhibiting signs of anxiety in fifth grade, I figured he had inherited an anxiety disorder from his dad's side. I had him see someone, and I had deemed it not a big deal. In high school it started to get worse, and that's when I pulled out the big guns, the best doctors I could find; whatever they cost didn't matter. I was saving my son. He had to get to college. He had to be successful. This whole anxiety thing had to be fixed. I had plans for him.

I found out about the pot in his junior year of high school. He had quit rugby but hadn't been taken off the roster and ended up with a random drug test required of athletes. The dean was as shocked as I was. My son swore it was a one-time thing. I had him see a drug counselor and an anxiety specialist; he did therapy and neurofeedback, anything I could find. Eventually he went off to college, the same school his three older siblings had attended, two of them still there, and came home on medical leave the week of finals in his first semester. No credits earned. More therapy, more ups and downs. One more attempt at college the following fall lasted six weeks then he was home again. More therapy and a well-respected clinic for social anxiety in Manhattan. He enrolled in the local community college so he could work on his anxiety while trying to be productive. Trying to help Patrick do what I thought he should do became a full-time, exhausting job with absolutely no rewards, that had eliminated all other relationships in my life and prevented any decent quality of life I had hoped for. I was sacrificing my entire existence, and he wasn't getting any better. I wasn't in denial, and I wasn't overtly enabling him. I was doing my best.

Finally, after a few months of sheer hell, after a particularly difficult few days, I had him taken to the psychiatric ER for eval-uation. The hospital had a beautiful, spa-like observation unit where they could keep people for seventy-two hours while they either sobered up or came down from a psychotic episode, so

that they could then be evaluated. I live on a little island facing
the hospital from across the river. My son's room happened to
face my apartment; from it, he could actually see my living room
TV. It was almost poetic, the universe telling him, "This is what
you're missing." When I picked him up the next day, without
being admitted, the discharging doctor looked at him and looked
at me and said to my son, "You need to have a conversation with
your mother."

At the time, he had been attending an intensive outpatient
program (IOP) for a social anxiety disorder. He went to his IOP,
spoke with his doctor there, and came clean, then he came home
and told me that he was addicted to Xanax, street Xanax, that
he was buying and using in addition to his prescription, as well
as abusing alcohol and anything else he could get his hands on.
I told him we'd find help. I called his doctor at the IOP, and she
told me that kids his age usually don't have lightbulb moments,
but he had, apparently, had one and I needed to get him help.
What that help looked like; she had no idea. She told me she would
make some calls and got back to me with the offer of a bed at the
hospital detox in three days.

He spent eight miserable days in detox, detox is no picnic,
which included a grand mal seizure and a short stint in the ICU.
It wasn't until he arrived at Caron and reality began to sink in,
that I was oddly comforted. The reason his anxiety wasn't getting
better was because we were treating the wrong thing. It wasn't the
answer I had hoped for, but it was an answer that made sense. I
now knew what we were dealing with, addiction, and that there
were people who knew what to do with that. I clearly wasn't one
of those people.

I share this with you because my ability to radically accept one,
that he was an addict, two, that I could not fix him, and three, that
other people might be able to help him fix himself, allowed me to
make the life-changing decision to do everything the professionals

told me to do and nothing they told me not to do. The most important thing they told me was to work on myself. So, I did, and my journey of recovery began. I began going to Al-Anon and attending parent support groups. I began to look at myself and my own behavior the way I hoped my son would look at his, and I learned how to make changes in my own behavior that resulted in a better life for me, just as I wished for him. I learned that just as my son was expected to work a program, so was I.

In working my own program of recovery and personal discovery and working with hundreds of parents and family members over the years, I can say with certainty that when we work on ourselves, our lives get better, and as our lives get better, we can put the struggles of others into proper perspective. We learn to accept what we can and cannot control and begin to understand the nature of addiction and mental health issues and how they can make really good people do really bad things. We begin to forgive, and we begin to heal. We learn how to control our responses to the behavior of others instead of trying to control the behavior of others. We learn to set healthy boundaries, focused on what is acceptable to us, and learn ways to enforce those boundaries that don't feel punitive, as it can be hard to punish a sick person. These are boundaries that allow us to feel safe and peaceful in our own lives. And as we start to step out of the chaos, we actually start to find real joy in our lives. Not a fragile peaceful or happy moment with an undertone of dread but a truly confident joy and peace that we know is within our control.

As you read this, remember, you didn't *cause* this disease, you can't *control* it, and there is no real *cure*—the three C's. I'll add two more C's: you can *contribute* to your misery caused by the disease, and you can *catch* it, as we often find our behavior mimicking the unhealthy behavior of the addict. They have their drug of choice and they become our drug of choice. This book is not about helping your child. It's about helping yourself. We've all done the best we could do at the time we did it. Hopefully, this book will help you find different ways to respond so that your best can be better. Let's meet ourselves where we are lovingly and move forward from here.

PART I

YOU, YOUR CHILD, AND THEIR BATTLE WITH THEIR DISEASE

We have no power in their war.

RADICAL ACCEPTANCE

"It is what it is. Accept it and move on from there."

One of the biggest challenges I've seen in parents is simple acceptance. Truth be told, I see this in most people regarding most difficult things. We want what we want the way we want it, and often that includes other people. We want our spouse to respond the way we want. We want our kids to fall into the future we have mapped out. We don't want it to rain on the day of the barbecue. These are big-picture things, some of which are clearly out of our control, the weather, for instance, and some of which can range from an irritant to a major disappointment. In recovery circles, both for families and addicts, the idea of accepting life on life's terms is fundamental to a healthy emotional life and personal recovery. When our child is suffering from a disease that only they can seek help for, the idea of acceptance can be much harder to swallow. How can I accept my kid ruining *his* own life? Let's look at what we really mean by acceptance.

First of all, what is it that we are accepting, and what does the fact that we accept it even mean? Let's be clear: accepting a fact of life, that our child is sick, is not the same as being okay with it. Acceptance is simply acknowledging the reality of a situation. "My daughter has blond hair and brown eyes and is an addict" can be a statement of fact. Resistance to acceptance can come in many forms from many places. I don't think I was in denial about my son. It was clear something was wrong; I was just wrong about what it was. I've spoken to many parents who beat themselves up because they didn't know what they were seeing. "I never knew a drug addict." "I had no idea how kids act on drugs." "All his friends were doing it, and I didn't realize that he had a problem." These are all phrases I've heard over and over again. You don't know what you don't know so forgive yourself and move on to knowing more. Radically accept that everything that brought you to this point has already happened, and the only way you can move is forward from here.

I worked with a mother who complained that her son's room was littered with water bottles filled with yellow liquid. The yellow liquid was urine because he spent all day shooting up in his room and wouldn't even get up to go to the bathroom. Everyone, including his brother, told her he was a drug addict. The drug paraphernalia was all over his room, in sight everywhere, but she was blind to it because accepting it meant she had to do something about it, and she was too paralyzed with fear to accept her reality. Some people refer to it "blissful denial." Trust me—there's no bliss in denial.

Two close friends of mine, after finally getting their kids sober enough so that their mental health issues could be accurately evaluated, received very difficult diagnoses that confirmed a whole new set of challenges that their child would be facing, even without substances. This is not uncommon, and in these cases the parent has to go through a whole new path of acceptance. It's never easy, but until we truly and radically accept what is, it will be impossible for us to deal with it effectively.

The reality of our child's life, their diagnosis, is often the first thing we need to accept, even if we initially don't want to hear it. The more challenging task is often what comes next—the fact that we cannot control it. We cannot cure our child's illness.

We cannot prevent the pain their illness causes without perpetu-ating their disease and making it tolerable. When their disease is tolerable, they won't get help. Intellectually, many of us may be able to accept that we cannot fix it. After all, haven't we already spent years trying our best, doing everything we could think of to make it better, to get them to see what they're doing to themselves, to convince them to get help, to get them to just stop and shape up and stop the madness???? Haven't we done all we could do and then we just do some more until we are doing the same thing over and over, running on autopilot, while nothing gets better and we just get worse? We've all been there. Some of us were willing to spin the wheels longer than others. Just as our addicts have their rock bottoms, we parents have them too, and sometimes, like our addict, when we hit it, we just dig a little deeper. We have to accept that we cannot cure our child. We can't fix them. We can support them in their recovery, but if they are not ready to recover, we can't fix it.

Another fact that we have to accept is that, in many cases, our child is actually an adult, and we have zero control over their behavior. In addition, as an adult, they are entitled to certain levels of privacy and respect. This can get convoluted in the throes of the chaos that addiction can cause. If they live at home, we can certainly set expectations and standards for our own home and give them a choice to respect these standards or leave, but if you find yourself going through your son's drawers looking for the drugs or bottles that you know you'll find, what's your goal? When he yells that you invaded his privacy, he's not wrong. You may logi-cally justify it because you did it out of desperation, not knowing what else to do, but did it serve any purpose? If he rummaged through your drawers looking for cash, you'd be irate, but he could justify it by being desperate too. This is where we begin to act like the addict, and we often end up being just as guilty of gaslighting them as they are of making everything our fault.

The reason that it's important to look at this, at how we are showing up in our relationship with the addicts, is that how we show up is the only thing that we actually can control. Later in this book, we will look at boundary setting and rules and how to determine acceptable behavior in our own homes and establish enforceable consequences. For now, I encourage you to begin to radically accept that your behavior has not always been helpful and that, if you're honest with yourself, no matter how logical and justified it may be, it has not always been behavior of which you're proud. That's okay. We've all been there. The more easily we accept what we can't control, the more quickly we can start focusing on what we can control, and that's where our own power starts to show.

WHAT RADICAL
ACCEPTANCE ALLOWS FOR

"Pain is inevitable. Suffering is optional."

We've talked about radically accepting the situation our child is in and the fact that we have to be responsible for our own behavior around it. Radical acceptance is a starting point and a pain point. It's really painful to fully admit how bad things are sometimes. It's painful to accept loss and disappointment. The truth is, when we don't accept the reality, when we stay in our child's disease and continue to try to mitigate it, we endure tremendous suffering. We put all our energy into trying to control something over which we really have no power, and then we are crushed and depleted when we don't get the results we want. Suffering is prolonged and chronic pain. According to Sheri Van Dijk, author of many books on dialectical behavior therapy (DBT), suffering is what happens when we refuse to accept the pain in our lives. The only way around pain is through it. We have to acknowledge it. We've all heard that time heals all wounds. The healing can't start until the feeling starts, for we can't heal what we don't acknowledge. The longer we wait to feel the pain, the longer we hold onto it. We need to get to know it and understand it. Suffering comes when we ignore the feelings and allow them to settle just beneath the surface, like a splinter lingering out of sight causing just enough pain to distract and eventually torture us until we dig away at it like a madman looking for relief. The longer the splinter stays, the greater the chance of infection and the longer our discomfort continues. Our body can't heal until the splinter is removed. Once we practice radical acceptance and we begin to address our pain, the healing begins, and the suffering begins to dissipate. We come to realize that we can feel the pain of our child's addiction *and* find joy in our own lives. We learn to be happy and sad at the same time.

Radical acceptance can be challenging and exhausting as well, but it ends up being the good kind of exhausting. I often help my clients through a phase of mourning as they begin to radically accept their child's condition and the fact that they themselves have no control over it. There is often a tremendous amount of grief, and parents sometimes judge their own grief as selfish. Don't judge yourself, please. Be kind and loving to yourself. Loss is hard, even if that loss is just the loss of a dream we had for our child. We are entitled to have dreams for them. Now we'll come to see that the dreams we hold for them will be more about how we want them to feel about their lives rather than the specifics of what they do with their lives. Parents sometimes describe it as a loss of hope. This loss of hope is usually a little convoluted. The hope that parents feel they lose is the hope that they can fix it so their child will have the life that they, the parents, imagined for them.

When we radically accept the disease, we also have to let go of our own vision for our child. Clearly none of us envisioned them becoming an addict, but they did, so we have to let go of all that stuff we saw for them before *and* allow ourselves to accept that although their lives will not take the path we expected and hoped for, there is always hope that their lives will be wonderful. There is always the hope that they will find recovery and go on to build joyful, meaningful, and fulfilling lives. It happens all the time.

Hope isn't always a good thing. Hope has a great reputation in our culture. It gives people the strength to carry on during difficult times and can serve as a purpose for perseverance in good times. However, there are times when hope can perpetuate our suffering. Hope can make us form attachments to outcomes and develop expectations for things over which we have no control, setting us up for disappointment, pain, and suffering. Like the adage about watching what we wish for, we have to be mindful of what we hope for.

When a client tells me they have lost hope, I ask, "What have you lost hope about?" What happens is they often run off a list of their own expectations about the outcomes for their child. They list several things around education, career, marriage, and family. After they list all this stuff, they inevitably settle on, "I just want them to get sober." As you really start to think about what you feel you've lost hope for you'll realize that the specifics of what you want for your child as far as education and career, for instance, start to feel trivial compared to the overwhelming yearning for your child to be well, to be able to handle life, and as long as your child is breathing, there is always hope that they will get better.

When we radically accept the pain in our lives and take our focus off the hope for certain outcomes that we still hold onto, we make space in our lives to find joy and see possibilities in life that we haven't ever imagined. Radical acceptance isn't about replacing trying to control their addiction with accepting it, and just accepting the pain. It's the way we start healing the pain. We begin to reflect on ourselves and how we are tending to all the other areas of our lives. Once we are able to see the pain in proper proportion to all the other stuff, as just one part of our lives, we can find relief from suffering. When the suffering begins to dissipate, we make room for all the good stuff to come in. As we begin to realize that we can have pain *and* joy in our lives, we begin to regain a sense of balance and peace. As we build the life we had hoped for ourselves, not one founded on pain but one that is a beautiful mosaic of life's experiences—the good, the bad, and the ugly—we build up our resistance to letting the suffering back in. When our comfort zone changes to a place of joy and peace, we find that we won't want to go back to those dark places. We won't want to get drawn into drama that we didn't create and can't control. We won't want the burden of responsibility for stuff that isn't ours. We will begin to use our power for good. We will start taking responsibility for the things in our life that we can control and showing up better for ourselves and for everyone around us.

Of course, this takes a lot of tough work, and it's not a journey you'll want to feel alone on. When you can look at this as a spiritual journey, where instead of fighting the reality of the world around you, you become a co-conspirator with the world around you, you get to create a new reality for yourself, and you will be able to look back on all the pain and understand the opportunities it presented.

LEARNING HOW TO SEPARATE YOUR CHILD FROM THEIR DISEASE AND YOU FROM YOUR CHILD'S DISEASE

"Your child is more than their disease."

In order for us, as parents, to start to engage in meaningful change, first we have to see what needs to be changed. Then we have to determine which of those things we actually have any control over. Once we focus on the things that we *can* control, we can get down to the work of changing them. Spoiler alert here: the only things we will find that we can change are how we are thinking and how we are behaving. Other things may need to change, but we can't control those things, so we have to concentrate on fixing ourselves.

It's also vital that we become aware of when we are in a state of chaos and are operating in crisis mode. When we are in these heightened states, our brains go into fight-or-flight mode, and our executive functioning skills become diminished. That means it becomes impossible for us to use our best decision-making skills. In order to make good decisions around difficult choices, we have to learn how to step out of crisis mode. It is possible to face a crisis without being in crisis mode. When working with parents,

I often have to point out that not everything is a crisis, but we become conditioned to react as if everything is. This leads to overwhelm and that can lead to bad decision-making or absolutely no decision-making because we become paralyzed with fear. In this section, we'll talk about understanding how the disease manifests in us and understanding how it results in unhealthy reactions and behaviors for both the addict and the parent.

There are hundreds of books on the science of addiction and the nature of addiction, what addiction does to the neural pathways, what it means to go through withdrawal, and tons of other technical information about the disease and the afflicted. Understanding the science is good if that's your thing, but it doesn't always help when you're in the room with your addict in crisis.

You can spend years ruminating over how this happened or why it happened, or from which gene pool the addiction tendency came. You can waste your time and energy trying to make sense of a senseless situation, trying to figure out what you did wrong or what their father did wrong or what his friends did wrong or what the school did wrong, or what your child did wrong. None of that helps when you're in the room with your addict in crisis either. We need to learn ways to stay calm and to de-escalate situations with our child when they cannot do this for themselves.

What I have found most helpful and what I have seen other parents benefit from most is an understanding of how the disease manifests, both in our child and in us. Being able to separate our child from their disease and, eventually, ourselves from their disease, is key to finding our own peace and serenity and can help us come to terms with the behaviors of our loved ones. A better understanding of the fact that their behaviors *are* their disease can lead to more empathy and compassion for their struggle, and, at the same time, help us differentiate between when we are supporting our children and when we are supporting their addiction.

Addiction is a disease of bad behaviors and it makes people behave terribly. It simply does, and the behaviors are quite predictable. The behaviors we will discuss may not apply to every addict, but they are bound to feel familiar. As parents, when we can accept the reality of the disease and manage our expectations around our children's behavior, we can prevent feelings of frustration and disappointment and avoid emotional reactions toward our children and instead take a step back and develop a more pragmatic approach, managing our emotions around the event, so that we can see all of our options on how to proceed and then respond more appropriately in the moment.

Understanding what is driving our children's behavior can go a long way in helping parents decide how to respond in any particular situation. If our son falls, scrapes his knee, and cries, we understand why he's crying and know how to respond. If our daughters get into a fight because one wore the other one's favorite sweater without asking, we also know how to respond, if at all. It's reasonable for a little boy to cry if he gets hurt. It's reasonable for someone to get angry if someone takes something of theirs without permission. We know the cause and we see a reasonable result. It all seems logical. With addiction, there is little logic but there is predictability, and knowing what to expect can allow us to be better prepared.

In this section, we will take a look at what we can expect from our child in active addiction and early recovery. We will also look at common reactions we may have so that we recognize what is acceptable and what is addiction-driven in our own behavior. We will likely see that our child's addiction is having a major impact on our own behavior, and we have to own that so that we can change it. Finally, we'll look at ways to apply this newfound awareness to managing our expectations around our child's and our own behaviors so that we can go into situations better prepared to respond in healthy ways.

WHO IS THIS PERSON THAT USED TO BE MY CHILD?

"Addiction can make good people do bad things."

I have never spoken to a parent of an addict who hasn't asked some form of this question, over and over. I've asked it myself. How the hell did this happen? What did I do wrong? How could he do this? How could he behave like this? How did I raise this? These are all reasonable questions. The problem is, they're not useful questions. They're almost rhetorical questions in that there is no satisfactory answer except for one. Your child behaves like this because they are an addict. You did not cause their addiction; therefore, you are not responsible for their behavior caused by their addiction. Your child's behavior is not a reflection of you. It is not your fault, and there is nothing you can do to control it. However, armed with radical acceptance and a better understanding of the predictability of their behaviors, you can create an environment where you are no longer complicit in it.

Without getting into the neuroscience of addiction, we must understand and accept that addiction is an actual disease. Your child is not choosing to use drugs or to drink out of the blue. They are in a chronic war with a chronic disease that tells them to use, and when they do use, it simply shows that they've lost the current battle. The ASAM, American Society of Addiction Medicine describes how addiction manifests itself through an inability to consistently abstain from the thing they are addicted to, an impairment in behavioral control, craving, a diminished recognition of significant problems with one's behaviors and interpersonal relationships, and a dysfunctional emotional response. Similar to other chronic diseases, addiction often involves cycles of relapse and remission. Our children have a defined psychiatric disorder, Substance Use Disorder/Addiction Disorder, according to the American Psychiatric Association's DSM, the manual that lists every recognized psychiatric diagnosis. Definitions of addiction often refer to biological, psychological, social, and spiritual manifestations due to malfunctioning circuits in the reward pathways of the brain. There is more going on than bad decisions. Their brains and bodies are betraying them, leading them to believe that they need harmful things in order to survive. Accepting that our child has a disease allows us to be less judgmental about their behavior and more compassionate about their pain. We can recognize behaviors as being unacceptable and refuse to accept said behaviors without anger and resentment. We can learn to detach emotionally from the situation so that we can respond appropriately.

On a side note, for the purpose of this book, I have chosen to use the terms addiction and addict rather than substance abuse disorder and someone who suffers from it. Please don't get caught up in the monikers. In AA meetings people stand up and say they are an alcoholic and a drug addict. Until they change that I am comfortable with the terms. The stigma won't disappear by relabeling the condition. It will begin to disappear when people normalize the disease and, as parents, when we can step out of shame and guilt and actually talk about our family struggles, we will begin to remove the stigma.

And for those of you who will not accept that it is a disease, the moniker doesn't matter. Don't get caught up in semantics. The behaviors are the same regardless of how we identify the underlying cause. Our children are causing themselves pain, and that pain is causing us pain. We need to learn healthy ways to deal with their behavior. The why of their behavior is not vital to us learning better ways of dealing with it.

Once we have accepted that our child has an actual disease and isn't just a disaster of a person by choice, it's vital for us to begin to make the distinction between our child and their disease. We must remember that our child is more than their disease. All their terrible behaviors are symptoms of their disease. Your child is sick, very very sick, and their illness causes them to behave in unacceptable, self-destructive, and painful ways. Their disease may define their behavior now, but they are more than the symptoms of their disease. Everything you've taught them and everything good is still there, even if it's locked away and difficult to access. It's crucial to understand and accept this so that we can manage to have compassion for them *and*, at the same time, not accept unacceptable behavior. We need to understand and accept this so that we can move out of anger and resentment toward them, which eats away at our own ability to have peace and into a space where we can feel compassion for our child, understanding that this is an incredible battle for them.

Addiction has caused them to wage war on themselves and they are in a constant state of battle, attacking themselves over and over. Think of an autoimmune disease where the body attacks itself. If our child had rheumatoid arthritis, we would have compassion for the pain and suffering. Our addicted child is constantly suffering. Anger and resentment are negative emotions, and they perpetuate our own misery. Compassion is so useful because it is a positive emotion. Compassion encompasses love and understanding. When we have compassion, we feel a warmth in our souls. When we have compassion, we are not playing the martyr or victim. We are operating from a place of being part of the bigger world. We are putting our own challenges aside for a moment and considering the challenges someone else is facing.

One of the hardest things for me to come to terms with early in my own journey was the level of pain that my son had been in. Even before he was actively using, under his joyful and lovable facade he was uncomfortable in his own skin. He never felt "normal." This is a common theme amongst addicts. They will often relate how they just never felt like other kids. The first time they used a substance was the first time they felt like they fit in, and their use of substances was usually immediately to excess. They might not have started drinking every day but when they did drink, it was to the point of blacking out. Some say it made them feel normal; some say it numbed the feeling of not fitting in. Different sides of the same coin. They will often say that they did not understand why they felt this way. Your child is in pain; it may seem self-inflicted, but that's not totally true. They have a disease that causes them to make decisions that cause them pain. It is an insidious disease that manifests in self-destruction.

When the disease takes hold, your child becomes obsessed with using. First, it's their drug of choice, and if they can't get that, then it's usually anything they can get. My son described it to me as an ache in his chest like he needed it to breathe. He clutched his sternum and hunched his shoulders as he said this to me. It was an image of incredible agony and desperation. Your child is in a constant state of desperation. They literally feel that their life depends on the next fix or the next drink. They become instinctual beings, caged and cornered by their own brains, and they go into survival mode, doing whatever it takes to be able to use. When the disease takes hold, things get ugly, and we need to be prepared.

PREDICTABLE BEHAVIORS
OF THE ADDICT

"Fool me once, shame on you.
Fool me twice, shame on me."

ADDICTS LIE.

They lie a lot, and they tend to lie about a lot of things. It becomes their default. They start creating their own version of reality and they start buying into it. Sometimes they lie to get what they want. Sometimes they lie because they carry so much shame and guilt that they can't face it. Remember, they are still themselves somewhere deep inside and know what they're doing is wrong. Lying is a symptom of their disease. It is painful for us to experience our child lying. It is painful to lose all trust in our child. It's also painful to fail to accept this inevitability and be constantly shocked and disappointed by it. Radically accept that the addict lies. Your child isn't a horrible person for it, they are a sick person doing horrible things and this is a symptom of their disease.

Why do we believe them? Because we want to. We want to believe that they didn't steal or aren't stoned. We don't want to accept the cold, harsh reality. We have to learn to manage our expectations. Our child will lie, and we shouldn't be shocked. We should be prudently on guard and expect to not be able to trust them when they are active and in early recovery. Eventually we may learn to trust their actions long before we trust their words.

ADDICTS MANIPULATE.

Hand in hand with lying, addicts do what they must for their survival, which they are convinced, by their disease, relies on their substance use. They will pit father against mother, grandparents against parents. They will use and abuse and alienate everyone who loves them and everyone they love. They will gaslight you by making you think that you are the problem and the cause of their own problems. They'll say it's your fault they use. They'll convince you to give them money one last time.

I had a client whose son was an active heroin user and would always ask his father for gas money to get to the methadone clinic. His father hated giving him gas money but felt like he couldn't not make sure his son got to the clinic. I pointed out that the purpose of methadone is to help someone to not use heroin. If his son was shooting up, he didn't need to get to the clinic! It seems obvious from the outside, but in the heat of the moment, we want to help and we want to believe them. We get sucked in. We allow ourselves to get manipulated and then blame our child when we are miserable and feel taken advantage of and we get angry and resentful. We need to own our own behavior. Fool me once, shame on you. Fool me twice, shame on me. We have to radically accept that our addict will try to manipulate us and be on guard against it. If we allow it and regret it, then we have to allow ourselves to learn from it. We have to own our own part in our own misery. If the flame is hot, we pull our hand away. If our child is in active addiction, we stay on guard.

I worked with this father on deciding whether giving his son gas money when the son was spending his own money on heroin, was supporting his son or supporting his addiction. Once he was able to see that he was supporting his son's addiction, the idea of saying no became a little easier. We also worked on alternative offers the father could make until he was ready to simply say no. The father decided he would get a gas can, fill it, and drop it off with his son if his son was truly out of gas. The father also came to realize that the gas was really the bait to draw the father into the habit of doing things the son should be doing for himself. When his son stopped getting a simple yes, he stopped asking altogether.

ADDICTS USUALLY CAN'T SHOW UP FOR LIFE IN NORMAL WAYS.

They are in a battle for their own survival. Don't expect them to behave and achieve like a normal person. My son got into college by the skin of his teeth and didn't last a semester. Other kids I know managed to finish college with good grades despite their substance abuse.

We often hear the term "functioning alcoholic." Some can manage their lives better than others. A lot of factors go into who our child becomes when they use. Their intellectual ability, co-occurring mental health disorders, trauma they may have suffered and many other factors play a role. As parents, we must be realistic about how we expect our child to show up. If the kid didn't make it through high school, we can't be surprised that he can't hold a job. If the kid is doing meth or heroin, they can't show up for their own kids. If the thirty-year-old daughter is a raging alcoholic, she probably won't be great about paying her bills or responding to wedding invitations, even if she manages to make it to work most days.

I had a lovely client who was upset that his daughter hadn't gotten the Covid vaccine. His daughter was shooting heroin. Obviously she wasn't focusing on her own health! We have to manage our expectations around our child's behavior in order to mitigate our own disappointment and resentments. When they are using, their lives are going to suck for the most part. It's sad. It's heartbreaking but it's inevitable. We have to radically accept this so that we can have some peace and stop setting ourselves up for constant disappointment

I worked with another client on managing expectations around his daughter's ability to hold a part-time job. His daughter had come home from college on medical leave for anxiety and was actively abusing pot and alcohol. He wasn't ready to accept that she would likely benefit from a residential program. Instead, if she couldn't go to school, he wanted her to get a job. The same issues that prevented her from succeeding in school also prevented her from holding a part-time job. It's illogical to think that something will change if nothing has changed. If his daughter couldn't show up for school because of drugs, she wasn't going to be able to show up for work.

I helped him come up with other more manageable expectations for his daughter so that he could get a better idea of the limits of her ability to show up for life, given her substance abuse. And I helped him proceed with these expectations with caution, understanding that if she was unable to comply with even the most basic expectations of personal care, then he may have to consider getting her a higher level of support. Instead of him just being tortured by the disappointment of her failings, he was able to create a plan to allow him to see the reality of the situation and to see all the choices he had around how to offer his daughter professional support.

ADDICTS ARE SOMETIMES VERY SMART, BUT IT DOESN'T MATTER; THEY'RE STILL ADDICTS.

So often parents will tell me how smart their kid is. If I had a dime for every time I heard "You don't understand; he's so smart."

I'm not criticizing; I used to say it. My son was and is a really intelligent guy. The unfortunate truth is that intelligence is weak armor against addiction. There's an important term used in the world of recovery: terminal uniqueness. The term is from AA, and it describes the alcoholic's belief that they are different from other alcoholics and that no one will ever understand them. It can serve as a barrier to recovery because they don't think that the recovery principles that helped others will apply to them. Sometimes it can come across as looking down on others with the same disease. Other times it is another manifestation of their hopelessness around actually being able to get better.

Although everyone is a unique individual, if you've ever sat in an AA meeting, you've heard the same story from the seventy-year-old businessman and the twenty-five-year-old college dropout. Same story, different details. We as parents often suffer from terminal uniqueness as well, and when you speak with other parents and family members of addicts, you'll see that we all develop the same destructive behaviors even though the details of our experiences are different. We think our situation is different, that our child is different from other addicts. We think they're better, smarter, or more educated, or that they're worse, they lie more, or are more manipulative than anyone else could possibly be.

I coached a father whose son had a terrible drinking problem. He smashed cars, had DUIs, and was taken out of his father's house by the police after assaulting his mother. Despite all this, the father still said his son had nothing in common with "those people" and that he would never go to a meeting in a church basement. Newsflash: his son was one of "those people." His son was an alcoholic despite his Ivy League degree. I gently challenged the father to show me how his son was different. How his son's DUIs were any different than anyone else's. How was assaulting his own mother in a drunken rage different from anyone else committing an assault? As is often the case, the crazy became normal.

The more the father looked at it objectively, separate from the pain this behavior caused him, he was able to see that his son was no different, and then he changed his own attitude toward his son's recovery.

Our child's stories may have different details, but their situations are not unique. We must radically accept that no matter how smart they are or which cultural or socioeconomic position they come from, an addict is an addict, and an alcoholic is an alcoholic. There are many ways to treat the disease and no aspect of a recovery program should be deemed beneath them. Church basements turn out the highest number of recovered people around the world, and the suggested donation is usually two dollars. I have clients who've spent hundreds of thousands of dollars on rehab for their kids and the kid won't stay clean. It's not about the program; it's about the person's willingness to do what it takes to build up the strength to fight the daily, lifelong battle to stay clean. When I sent my son off to rehab, I handed my precious, broken baby boy to a bunch of recovering addicts and recovering alcoholics and prayed they could help fix him. I realize now that all they could do was teach him how to fix himself.

ADDICTS ARE RESOURCEFUL.

When I got a call on day three of a twenty-eight-day program that my son was checking himself out, I was in a panic. They suggested that since I owned his phone, I should not authorize them to return it to him. I said, "Well, I technically own his underwear too; should I send him out naked?" They advised that what usually happens is they wander around for a while and when they realize they have nowhere to go, they call the center and ask to be picked up. I said, "How is he going to call you if he doesn't have a phone?" His case manager responded, "He's a resourceful kid; he'll figure it out." That was a white-light moment for me. Obviously, he was a resourceful kid, he had figured out how to buy drugs. A few hours later, some of the longest hours of my life, he did just that. He borrowed a phone from someone mowing their lawn, called me, and called the rehab. I'm fighting back tears as I write this. Tears of relief, even after all these years, that it turned out that way, and tears of sorrow for all the pain this terrible disease causes millions of addicts and all the millions of people who love them. But the lesson is important for parents when dealing with the lies and manipulation we face. If a kid can get heroin, he can get gas money. If she can buy drugs, she can buy groceries.

We have to be vigilant and remember that just because our child is in an uncomfortable situation as a result of their own behavior, we do not have to fix it. More often than not, if we step back, they figure a way out of it. They are resourceful. We may not approve of their way out, but we can't control it, and it isn't our responsibility anyway.

A client of mine has a brother who is an active alcoholic. Her brother called, demanding money for bills he had due. My client said she would think about it and called me. I suggested that she take her time responding and wait to call her brother until after the weekend, giving herself time to decide if she would help and how. When she called her brother back a few days later, her brother declared that he had already found the money he needed. The next time it happened, my client told her brother right off that she wouldn't give him the money and ended the conversation. It wasn't her problem to solve, and her brother had proven his own resourcefulness.

That's the thing with resourcefulness. All it means is they can get what they want. Asking us for help is just one option they use. If that doesn't work, they move on to the next option. We don't have to help them and if we do, then we risk becoming complicit in their unhealthy behavior. Remember, when they say they need your help with something that is their responsibility, it's okay to say no. More often than not, we should say no. Because here's the thing, when their resourcefulness starts to run out and they run out of options, staying in their addiction can become even more uncomfortable than fighting it, and they may actually seek help.

Understanding and accepting that addiction is a disease of bad behaviors helps us step out of the prolonged suffering that the "why" questions can cause and into a more realistic view of what we're dealing with. I am teaching you different strategies to deal with very complex situations. When we can anticipate how someone will behave, we can manage our expectations to avoid an emotional response and plan, in advance, our healthiest response. We need to stop constantly reacting and instead learn how to respond. We do that by slowing down. Our power lies in the time between the trigger and our response. A knee-jerk reaction is not a power move. Taking time to think allows us to respond. Understanding what to expect by understanding how the addicts behave gives us that time by preventing the emotional shock and disappointment of the behavior. It takes away the shock value so we can think. Every little thing stops feeling like a crisis. This is an important concept because our thinking becomes as crazy as theirs and our reactions to their behaviors become destructive on their own.

WHO IS THIS PERSON
THAT USED TO BE ME?

"The crazy became normal."

It's one thing to wonder how our child's life can be so horrid, but when we look at our own lives, we realize that our own life often mirrors the insanity of our addict's. We don't spend all day thinking about using, but we spend all day thinking about our child using. Our child has their drug of choice and they often become our drug of choice, and we think about them incessantly. Just as we have to separate our child from their disease, we have to begin to separate ourselves from our child's disease as well. We are more than our addicted child. Chances are that we have made some good choices in our lives and have many good things in our lives. All that counts too. We must not define ourselves and our lives by our greatest suffering. Our child is at war with an enemy that can only see them. The enemy doesn't see us. The enemy isn't interested in anyone but the addict. We have to stop trying to do battle with it. We can't hurt it. We can't control it. We can't fix our child. We can't fight this war for them. When a child falls down a well, nobody crawls down into the well with them. They stay up top and strategize how to get them out. Going to war with our child's addiction on their battlefield is futile. It puts us down in the well with our trapped kid and then we're both stuck and can't get out.

We have our own battle to fight against the effect we allow our child's addiction to have on us. We have our own battle against the mirroring behaviors that we've developed as a result of trying to control our child's addiction. When we spend time trying to control our child's disease, we crawl into the trench alongside them, and we have to get out of the trench before we can have any hope of being able to help them. We have our own war to wage and many changes that we have to make in our own thoughts and behaviors in order to win back our own battleground.

When my son started to struggle, I went into what I call machine mode. It's what I used to do in times of crisis. I got laser-focused on doing what I thought needed to be done. I was always kind of proud of my ability to handle crises. The problem was, unlike a normal crisis that comes on suddenly and is easily identifiable, his addiction came on slowly. It started with anxiety and stress. His grades started falling. He was having trouble focusing. I immediately had him see the best doctors I could find. I spoke to his teachers about his stress to troubleshoot ways to mitigate it.

The thing about addiction that caught me off guard is just how insidious a disease it is. At first, the signs can look like normal adolescent and teenage struggles. They can start to struggle a little here and a little there, and before you know it, the struggle becomes the norm, and by the time the struggle becomes a major problem, even the major problem starts to feel normal. Before I realized it, my entire life had become consumed by my son's struggles, and I got so pummeled by the waves of despair, disappointment, and fear that I no longer knew which way was up. I might have been in machine mode, but the machine was totally malfunctioning. I had no clue what needed to be done. I didn't understand what I was dealing with, other than something horrible.

The result was not only that I was behaving like someone I didn't know, but I was so far down the well with him that I didn't even see how out of control my own life had become. I had left my job. I ended a relationship. I wasn't seeing any of my friends. My older kids were dreading coming home from college because I had become so exhausted and full of despair that I looked at their coming home as a relief so that they could take over trying to fix their brother. When I look back what I realize now is that I had become completely powerless in my own life. I had relinquished all of my power to my son's addiction, and I had to get it back.

How many of you can relate to this? A feeling of powerlessness is pervasive in the world of parents of addicts. We may not be able to think of it that way because we're too crazed to step back and examine the state of our lives, but when we do, we realize how utterly depleted we have become. The good news is that if we gave it away, then we can take it back.

My family is big into superheroes so I like to use a Superman analogy. Superman has x-ray vision. No questions, he knows it and we know it. It's one of his superpowers. However, if he tries to see through lead it doesn't work. It doesn't mean he no longer has the power; he's just using it in a way that it doesn't work. When he looks at drywall, he sees right through it. We each have a tremendous amount of power over our own lives. When we try using that power over our child's addiction, it simply doesn't work. When we try using it to control our child's behavior, it simply doesn't work. We don't have the power to control this. When we start using our power to control our own behavior, we feel the full strength of our own power. When we start focusing on what *we* are doing instead of on what other people are doing, we start to see how responding to situations differently can dramatically change our lives. We are responsible for our own happiness. We are responsible for finding a way through difficult situations so that we can be okay. We can't blame anyone else for what we allow in our own lives, even our addict. The addict is just doing their thing. They're not doing it *to* us; they're just doing it. We are making it our own. We are relinquishing our power. We are surrendering to an enemy that doesn't even know we exist. We need to reclaim our power and use it in the only way it actually works. We need to fix ourselves.

PREDICTABLE BEHAVIORS
OF PARENTS

*"Our child becomes our drug of choice and
we become obsessed ourselves."*

Just as our child's behaviors change when their addiction takes
over, our own behaviors change because of our child's addiction
as well. And like our children, our own behavior patterns become
predictable. Many of these behavior patterns arise when dealing
with any alcoholic, whether it's a parent, sibling, or child. Some
of us can trace these behaviors back to a time before our child
was struggling because the source was an addict or alcoholic that
came into our lives before our child. Either way, consider these
patterns and whether they describe you. If they do, then realize
that you are contributing to your own misery and you have the
power to change these behaviors so that you can be contributing
to your well-being instead.

As you read this, please don't read it with any judgment. It
isn't written with any. Be gentle with yourself. Be kind to yourself. It's okay if we're a little broken; we've been to war. We've
been watching our kids in battle and it's heartbreaking. When we
come back to ourselves, we can heal. We can grow from it and
learn from it. Just as scar tissue is tougher than skin, we can end

up better and stronger. No matter what. If we learn how to heal and develop resiliency, we will not only survive but we will thrive.

I didn't know how I would possibly survive my son's addiction, but I did as I was told and I stepped back from focusing on his behavior and began to focus on mine. My life is more than I ever could have imagined. I have become stronger. I have a better understanding of my role and opportunity in the world. I can be happy and sad at the same time. I can feel hope and disappointment. I can take my struggle and use my experience to help someone else who is struggling. It wasn't easy. I had a lot of reckoning to do with myself, but I also decided that I would hold myself to the same standard I held my son. I did for myself all the things I hoped he would do for himself. I went to Al-Anon meetings, I went to parent support groups, I forgave myself, I forgave others, I learned better ways of being, and I healed. I learned to mind my own business and just concern myself with my own behavior. I was kind and gentle with myself, but I held myself accountable for my role in my happiness. This is what we all need to do in order for us to get our lives back. But first, let's look at some things we may need to stop doing.

WHAT WE NEED TO
LEARN TO STOP DOING

"It only takes one person to change a dynamic."

Just as this disease results in predictable behaviors in our children, we also develop predictable behaviors. Since our behaviors are the only thing we can control, it's important that we recognize them so that we can stop exhibiting them. We must focus on our own behaviors and stop doing things that are not helping our kids and are making our own lives worse.

STOP TRYING TO FIX AND CONTROL

"Bless them, change me."

Control is a funny thing. It often looks like love. It often looks like caring. It often looks like making sure everything works out. We like to help; it's who we are. We're fixers. We're problem solvers. We may not think of ourselves as controlling if we don't see ourselves as domineering or bossy. We may pride ourselves in our perfection around certain things: running a tight ship at home or being super productive at work. We want the laundry done, and our son is taking too long, so we do it for him. They don't stack the dishwasher "right," so we do it ourselves. We don't delegate at work because we know how it should be done and don't trust anyone else to do it "right." We do it and "we don't mind."

We previously discussed identifying obvious things that we can't control, like the weather and other people's behaviors. Here we'll look at subtle ways that our desire to control the big picture, the outcome, can often create our own form of chaos where we find ourselves playing the martyr or the victim disguised as the loving mother or the overworked, constantly busy parent.

As parents, some of us get so used to fixing things that we find ourselves lost when we can't. In reality, fixing things is not a caring, loving thing to do when it comes to older kids and adults. Don't wear "fixer" as a badge of honor. We fix to make it easier on ourselves and we fix to control the outcome; it's that simple. We may do it with our spouses and children. We want it our way, so we do it our way, and in doing so, prevent our children from learning how to do it themselves and which way is best for themselves. We aren't thinking of the other person when we are doing things for them that they should be doing for themselves. We're thinking about ourselves and how we want things to be and making sure we control the end result. If we've done this their whole lives, we may also be sending a message that we don't think they're capable of doing these things, further feeding the disease monster that already tells them they're incompetent and not worthy. Fixing = controlling. We have to stop!

I had a client who drove her adult daughter, who had a car, to and from her therapy appointments. I asked her why she was driving her. She said she wanted to make it easier for her so she didn't have to park. I asked her what they talked about on their way to the therapist and on the way home. No surprise, on the way to the therapist, the mother would go over what she should be talking about and on the way home, she would try to get her to say if she had discussed what had been suggested. I'll never forget the sound she made when she heard herself and realized she was driving her to try to control how her daughter's private therapy sessions went! Again, any of us with children or spouses in therapy have probably made suggestions and pried a little as well. Let's own it and stop it. It's not caring; it's controlling.

The other thing that our effort to control things can do is cause us to play the role of both martyr and victim. When we become obsessed with fixing and controlling our addict, we often expect others to pick up the slack in our own lives. Another client complained that her husband left her with all the responsibility for the adult addict daughter. The daughter didn't live with them. I asked my client if her husband left her with the responsibility or if she took on responsibilities that didn't belong to her. Should either of them take on these responsibilities? The answer was no. So, my client was doing things that she shouldn't have been doing, resentful that her husband wasn't helping her with these things that she shouldn't be doing, and then getting further pissed that he wasn't being super helpful with all the stuff she should have been doing but wasn't because she was busy with the stuff she shouldn't have been doing. If it sounds crazy, it's meant to! This is what we become when we try to control things that aren't in our control and try to fix things that aren't ours to fix.

My client deemed herself both the victim and a martyr, but both were of her own making. None of this is said with any judgment or accusation. Dealing with our kids' addiction and illness is painful. Seeing how we may have been contributing to the pain can be tough. We need to be gentle with ourselves and keep remembering that we did the best we could. Being willing to accept the truth of my son's addiction, even though I didn't want it to be true, allowed me to focus on what I could do to move forward, for me and my whole family. In the same way, I was eager to learn what I had been doing wrong because if I was doing it, then I could control it, and after learning about all I couldn't control,

I was happy to identify what I could. So yes, bring it on; tell me all the ways I've been screwing up so I can fix that.

As you go through this book, I encourage you to adopt a similar attitude. This is your way out of the chaos. Own your faults and your missteps and do better moving forward. You can't fix what you won't admit is broken. You've been the best parent you can be. Now eat some humble pie, give yourself a huge loving hug, and change what you need to change. You're not alone in this. I've done it, millions of others have done it, and now it's your turn. It's your opportunity. You get to make your life better!

STOP BEING CODEPENDENT AND ENMESHED

"Stop breathing out when they breathe in."

Codependency can often become a fundamental part of the parent-child addict relationship. The parent-addict relationship becomes codependent when the parent becomes so obsessed with the addicted child that the parent completely forgets about their own needs and desires and focuses solely on the needs of the addict child. The addict child then becomes dependent on the attention from the parent and a vicious cycle of dysfunction ensues. The parent does everything for the child; the child does nothing for themselves because the parent does it all, and the child becomes incapable of doing anything for themselves because they have never had to, resulting in the parent feeling like they have no choice but to do everything for the child, even if the child is a forty-five-year-old man. Often, a codependent person will find that in most of their relationships, they create a dynamic where others end up dependent on them because they need to be needed.

Although it didn't originate with her, codependency is a term most associated with Melody Beattie, author of the bible of codependency *Codependent No More* and the daily reader accompaniment,

The Language of Letting Go. The book talks about how she came to "discover" codependency. She was in addiction recovery herself and working for a rehab program. She was asked to lead a support group of family members of the addicts and quickly realized that they were all as "crazy" as the addicts. I'm paraphrasing here, but she basically said that the alcoholics had an excuse to be this way; this group was this way sober. I burst out laughing when I first read her introduction. I believe in laughter as good medicine and a necessity for life, so you go, Melody! A sure sign of a healthy person is the ability to laugh at yourself. Let's face it—as parents we have put on a bit of a show.

My issue with labels around behavior is that they can be too defining and that can cause people to resist not just the moniker, but the lessons to be learned from the behavior. Not everyone who has exhibited codependent behaviors is a lifelong codependent. Some of us may have reacted to our child's addiction in a way that we don't react to other relationships in our life. I think it's important to know what behaviors to look for and learn ways to correct them. Beattie's books are on my suggested readings, but they may not resonate with you. They didn't, for instance, resonate as much with me. Codependency didn't play a huge role in my relationships, but it comes up often in my clients' lives. There are many consistencies in the world of addicted children and their parents, but in the end, we are all different and just as there is no single right answer on what's best for each of us, no single label defines us.

Enmeshment is a similar beast and I see it most with parents who have dealt with the struggle for a long time. Where codependency is an emotional dynamic, enmeshment is more of a boundary issue with no sense of personal boundaries between the parent and the child, and it can go both ways. When parents are enmeshed, they know every detail of their child's life and become involved in every detail of their child's life. There's no sacred privacy. And there's no room for either to breathe different air. One inhales and the other exhales. I also see this a lot when the child had a mental diagnosis at a young age, so the parent went into protection mode years before the addiction kicked in. For others, the parent and child have been in this dance of codependency, saving and needing to be saved for so long that they have lost sight of where one life begins and the other ends. You know how sometimes a person can lose a lot of weight, but if you see them every day, you may not notice? You go two weeks without seeing them and suddenly, it's like, *whoa, what a difference.* I've observed a similar response with enmeshed parents. Sometimes they are so close with their active addict child that they start to forget how sick the son or daughter is. The dysfunction becomes so familiar that it starts to feel normal.

When parents forget how sick their child is and the lines between normal and dysfunction, acceptable and unacceptable, become blurred, they often hold unrealistic expectations for how the child should be functioning. Another client was fully enmeshed with her forty-six-year-old heroin-using daughter. They would text each other or speak every day. The mother would reach out mostly to make sure the daughter was alive, and the daughter to make sure she could get what she wanted from the mother. The encounters were usually unpleasant. There was no real feeling behind the words and the mother often felt drained after speaking with her daughter, yet the thought of not texting or speaking with her every day was terrifying to her. Her day, her mood, and her relationship with her husband and other son and daughter were totally dependent on the mood of her addicted daughter, the one using heroin and in a terrible mood almost all the time. It sounds insane but it felt normal to her, unpleasant but acceptable. That's one of the scariest things about this disease. It makes the insane feel normal, even for those of us that don't have it. I worked with the mother on breaking this pattern of immersing herself in her daughter's world of drug use, so that the mother could begin to enjoy all the other things in her life. The mother was living the life of the addict without ever using drugs herself.

We need to create space between ourselves and our addicted child. There's a saying that we have to step back so that they can step up. It's unfair for us to burden our struggling child with the responsibility of our own emotional well-being. It's unfair to them and it's unfair to ourselves. We are putting our emotional well-being into the hands of someone else. Someone who can't take care of their own emotional well-being. We need to find healthier ways to feel fulfilled and to have a purpose in life other than fixing our child. We need to stop focusing on how they are behaving and start looking at how we are behaving. We need to give them space away from us and give ourselves space away from them.

STOP ENABLING THEIR DISEASE

"Support your child, not their disease."

Enabling is another word that can't be left out of a conversation about addiction. I don't like the word and I particularly dislike the label of enabler. It's almost always someone else accusing another of being the enabler, usually one parent toward the other, or the guilt-ridden, self-professed enabler who claims blame for all the horror. Any of us who have an addicted child have enabled at one time or another, some maybe more than others, but we've all done it. It's the nature of the beast. Like everything else, it's important to recognize when we do it so that we can stop doing it. And, like many other things, addiction blurs the lines of normal behavior, causing the same action to be okay in some circumstances and enabling in others.

If you look up *enabling* in the dictionary it has a very positive vibe. You're activating or giving them authority to do something.

Unfortunately, in the world of addiction, the thing that you're giving them the authority to do is either less than they should be doing, or worse, destructive things. In addiction terms, it actually rewards bad behavior. When you do things for people that they should be doing for themselves, and when you protect people from the consequences of their own actions (sounds like fixing), there is little incentive to activate the change that is needed for them to get help. In other words, to quote a dear client of mine, you make their addiction tolerable. We don't change things we can tolerate. If we keep the addict comfortable, we prevent them from wanting to change. Of course, we exhaust ourselves in the process by cleaning up the messes they create, funding tickets and lawyers, making excuses for their absences, and, most painfully, watching them sink deeper into their disease.

What are examples of enabling? For the addicted child, it's doing anything for them that they should be doing themselves; doing their laundry, making them food, buying them takeout if the house is full of food, supporting them financially, accepting unacceptable behavior in your own home, fixing the car after an accident, allowing them to use the car after an accident, giving them a car in the first place if they were already acting up, paying for the best lawyer to get them out of a DUI, calling your cop friend to make sure they don't get arrested. A tough fact to swallow: if you're their source of money and they're using the money you give them to buy drugs and alcohol, then you become complicit in their drug use. If you look at this sample list, the first few things a thirteen-year-old should be able to do for themselves; that being said, it's totally normal for a family to eat dinner together cooked by one of the parents. It's also totally normal for kids to have an allowance, hopefully dependent on completing certain chores, and if the car gets banged up, parents often fix it. The difference is that we have to parent our addicts a little differently than we might our other, "normal" kids, if we have them. The truth is, we probably started parenting our addict differently a long time ago, when the first signs of trouble cropped up. It might have been that we noticed they struggled more in social situations or developed anxieties our other kids didn't face. Chances are we started protecting them way before they started using and as they started using, we just felt the need to protect them even more. Even if it didn't feel normal, it may have felt right, and we couldn't see another way of doing it.

We have to understand that helping our addict doesn't look like helping our other kids, and the things we do for our other kids may actually harm the addict. My addict is the youngest of my four children. Each of his siblings came home for a few months after they finished their degrees. By the time my son finished his twelve-month rehab, he was doing really well. He was working his program, going to school and working a part-time job, supporting himself financially, and making me as proud as his siblings had, yet I was told not to let him come home to live. He wasn't asking to move back home; he had gotten the same message I had from his recovery program, but as a mother, it just didn't seem fair. I spoke with his case manager and expressed my concerns. Bill was a no-nonsense guy and I appreciated his somewhat sarcastic demeanor. He said, "Look, he has to know that he can do it on his own. He needs to live on his own, pay his own bills and figure it out for himself. If he wants to return to the city to finish school in six months or a year, you can revisit it, but for now, he needs to do this."

Patrick not moving home wasn't about me being fair or not. It wasn't about me at all. It was about him doing what he needed to do and building the confidence in himself that he could do it. When we enable, it's like fixing; we make it about us instead of our kids. It's hard to see our child taken to a psych ward or put into a police car. It's hard to sit and watch their laundry pile up or refuse to give them cash at will and deal with their complaining.

These things are hard for us, yes, but it's not about us. If our goal is to help our child, then these things are crucial. Call them necessary evils if you must, but sometimes they simply must be done. Tough love isn't about being tough with our kids. It's about making the tough decisions when they're too sick to make them. It's about looking at the tough, hard reality of their lives and deeming it unacceptable for us to participate. The sad truth is, we can, in some ways, love our kids to death if we allow ourselves to become complicit in their disease. We have to learn ways to not participate in their addiction. We often do things for them because we think they can't do them for themselves when they've never actually been given the opportunity to try. We have to allow them to think that we believe in them so they may see the possibility of believing in themselves.

Being able to separate our child from their disease is crucial to allowing us to see when we are supporting our child and when we are supporting their disease. Rather than think in terms of enabling, simply ask, "If I do this, whatever the 'this' is, am I supporting my child, or am I supporting their unhealthy behavior?" We can have compassion for their struggles without taking responsibility for their struggles. We can agree to take our child out to dinner without giving them money for food. We can allow them to be late for school rather than take it upon ourselves to make sure they get up and out on time. We can let their laundry pile up until they can't stand it anymore. We can be happy even if they are sad. We can give up trying to control things that are not ours to control. We can stop doing things for them that they should be doing for themselves and allow for the possibility of the things simply not getting done. We have to give them the opportunity to feel consequences. Consequences promote growth. Consequences promote learning. Our preventing them from feeling consequences promotes stagnation and enables their addiction to rule their lives.

STOP GIVING ADVICE

*"We don't know what's best for ourselves; we
certainly don't know what's best for them."*

One of the things I see all the time is our tendency as parents to give the same advice over and over to our children. "You know what you should do…" is probably the most used phrase in our language. Most people are great at giving advice, and often, it is advice that they themselves can't follow. My mother used to say, "Do as I say, not as I do." We always seem to somehow know what's best for everyone else. When it comes to our addicted child, getting sober is an obvious thing they should do, but telling them that over and over can be torturous for us. The problem is not the message; the problem often lies in the delivery of that message and the messenger themself.

Saying things like "You need to stop" or "Just stop" can end up, in the best case, useless and, in the worst case, causing more harm than good. Telling someone who can barely function that they should get a job or go to college is ludicrous. Telling them how they're screwing up their lives is not motivating; it's just stating the obvious. Our kids are sick. They know they're screwing up their lives, and they are so sick that they sometimes don't care and often don't see how it could be possible to stop. They are at war inside themselves and when we as parents repeat the same advice, often in a punitive manner, over and over, we accomplish nothing except to prove to them that we don't understand and to cause incredible frustration for ourselves. Here again, bringing on our own misery and blaming it on them.

I guarantee that if you are reading this book, you have probably already given your best possible advice multiple times. I ask you to be honest with yourself. Has it stopped your child from using drugs? I'll bet heavily the answer is *no*. And now think about how you feel after sharing your brilliant thoughts with your child, whether you shared them screaming at the top of your lungs or calmly and compassionately in a moment of peace. Do you feel relieved that they finally get it, that they finally understand and will stop? Or do you feel crushed, angry, frustrated, resentful, or all the above because no matter how you say it, they don't seem to hear you?

I've been there. So many of us have. We gave our best until we had nothing left to give and drove ourselves crazy doing so. The bottom line is that when our kids are actively using drugs and alcohol or dealing with any other kind of addiction, there is little they can actually hear from us, and even less they can actually learn from us. We are not the right messengers. We don't know what our kids need to do to get sober. We know they need to get sober, but we don't know what that should look like for them. I've worked with many parents who are sober themselves and the level of frustration that they, knowing what they know firsthand, still have no idea how to help their child is heartbreaking. Each person has their own journey. I know many people that got sober in prison and say going to prison saved their lives. Could you imagine that? I have a friend who said her parents were so incapable of offering the support and structure that she needed that jail was the first place she ever had structure and would never have gotten sober if she hadn't served time. I'm not promoting prison as a great solution, but I am saying that we don't know what moment is going to cause our child to want help, or if that moment will ever come. We have to stop acting like we know what's best. We have to radically accept that we don't know how to fix them because it is impossible for us to fix them. They have to fix themselves, and more importantly for us, we have to fix ourselves.

Once we take advice-giving out of our conversations, there will be a lot of silence. Silence can be very good. Silence can be healing. It can allow people to breathe and process. When we stop trying to do the impossible, we leave room for seeing what is possible. We love our children fiercely, even if we hate them at times. We may feel like we want to kill them but that's because we love them and had expectations borne of love for them, for our relationship with them, and what we thought their lives might look like.

So how do we speak to someone we love who can barely hear us? I remember hearing a sober woman speak one time. She had been sober for many years and was a beautiful woman. She had been a star athlete in high school, and a Division 1 athlete in college until she wasn't anymore because her addiction took over. She addressed a group of parents and I'll never forget her saying, "I couldn't hear any advice my parents gave me. The only thing I remember is that my mother would always say, 'Lilly, you were meant for more than this.'"

We can tell our children we love them even when they're breaking our hearts. We can tell them that we know they are meant for more. We can tell them that we know they are suffering, and we will support any effort to get help. We can tell them that help is possible, that they are not alone, and that there are people who can help them. We can speak compassionately for their sake and for our own. We're all in pain. Instead of giving them unsolicited advice, we can start taking our own advice.

Although we'll discuss boundaries a little later in the book, it's also important to bring them up here. When our children are in the throes of active addiction and unable to hear our words of love and wisdom, sometimes the only way to get through to them is by making them feel something, and that something is usually discomfort. After all, discomfort is the only thing that promotes change. We generally don't change comfortable things, even if they don't work for us anymore. Think of the comfortable old t-shirts we won't get rid of regardless of the holes. Even with clothes, we usually only keep them until they are no longer comfortable. When our kids cannot hear our advice or hear us

talking about the consequences of their use and how they are ruining their lives, boundaries allow our children the opportunity to
feel the consequences of their behaviors. We don't set boundaries
to change someone else's behavior. We set boundaries to protect
ourselves and preserve the quality of our own lives. However,
our children have often taken over many aspects of our lives and
homes and made themselves comfortable in this world where their
addiction rules the home. As boundaries start to help us rebuild
our home the way we want it, the consequences of violating these
boundaries can become quite uncomfortable for our kids. I often
say that many kids get help not when they reach rock bottom but
when their parents do.

The thing to always remember when speaking with our
addicted kids is that actions speak louder than words. Boundaries
are a language we have to learn and are often the only language
our addicted child can understand. Resist the urge to tell them
what to do and focus on what you're going to do to get your own
life back, something we'll be talking about later in the book.

STOP WORRYING ABOUT THEIR
TRIGGERS AND RELAPSES

"We have far less power over this than we think."

A dear friend of mine tells the story of having dinner with his
son once his son was sober, and asking his son, with complete
love and a yearning to understand what had gone wrong, if there
was anything he could have done differently to stop his son from
using. His son looked at him from across the table and shook his
head a bit and said, "Do you still think you had any power?"
That's a humbling and honest response. We have no power over
our children or their disease. We cannot control their disease.
As frustrating and difficult as this is to accept, it's also freeing.

When we don't have the power, it means we don't have the responsibility either.

My clients often talk about walking on eggshells in their homes and around their children, for fear of upsetting their child. Does that sound familiar? A trigger is something that causes a response usually associated with negative emotions. We need to understand that the addiction, the disease itself, is the main trigger. The disease causes our child to feel broken, not whole. This discord inside of them, the hole in the soul as it's often called, is what makes them drink and use drugs. Using substances becomes their only coping mechanism to help them either bear life or get numb to it. Their use becomes such an integral part of their existence that they are often unaware of their own triggers. They use because of everything that happens around them. The continued use causes toxic behaviors in both them and eventually in us. These toxic behaviors and the dynamic they produce in their relationships and lives cause more stress and become identified as triggers. Triggers didn't cause them to become addicts; they are a result of being addicts and having drugs as their only coping tool.

It's important that we understand the nature of triggers because when parents live in constant fear of triggering their child, they begin to operate from a state of fear and make decisions from a state of fear and end up allowing their child's disease to make their decisions for them in an effort to tame the beast. The next thing you know, everyone is walking on eggshells and the parents have lost all power over their own lives. If we look at triggers as another part of the disease, and we accept that we have no control over the disease, then we have to accept that we have no control over their triggers. We cannot cause our kids to use more, just as we can't control them to stop. We don't have that power. We have to understand this, because the number one enemy of healthy boundaries is fear of triggering our child and causing them to use more. Fear causes us to avoid confronting them on things that we may need to confront them on and dissuades us from refusing to engage when they push for an unhealthy confrontation.

For those of you who may have a child that is already sober or in the early stages of sobriety, the same goes for relapses. We have no responsibility for whether someone relapses or not, and neither does anyone else except the sober person. Taking responsibility for a child's potential relapse can wreak havoc on a family. I've spoken to so many parents who used to have their child under a microscope, and once the child gets sober, they put each other under a microscope and tell me that if the husband keeps this up it's going to cause the son to relapse or if the mother doesn't stop, the daughter is going to use again. A person relapses because they are not working a strong enough program to stay sober, period. They don't relapse because they get angry or because something bad happens. They relapse because they can't stay sober. We, as parents, can learn how to best support their efforts to stay sober if we are involved in their lives. Things like deciding not to serve alcohol at family functions, especially during early sobriety, is a reasonable show of support for many families. But truly, the best thing we can do for our child is to turn the microscope on ourselves and pay the most attention to what we are doing, how we are behaving, and how we are showing up in our own lives. The more honestly we can look at ourselves, the better we will be able to see what we have to do differently and the healthier we will become. And like I always say, the healthier we are, the better we can be for everyone.

We'll talk more about this when we talk about picking and choosing our battles, but we have to be keenly aware of when we are operating in a state of fear. Our walking on eggshells is our reaction to our own triggers. Our child's behavior triggers us to fear a confrontation that will cause them to use more. It also can trigger a whole host of other emotions. I have one client who had been dealing with her daughter's addiction for so long that she would always say, "I don't care anymore. I just don't want the fight." We dove deeper and determined that, of course, she still cared. She was simply utterly exhausted, emotionally drained, and afraid to admit she cared because she was so afraid of her daughter's addiction. Her daughter's behavior caused her to feel afraid, sad, responsible, frustrated, and bewildered. I helped her manage her fear and rebuild her own emotional strength so that she had the energy to respond in a more rational manner and not allow herself to be triggered by her daughter. She came to realize that shutting down and walking on eggshells had become her dominant coping skill, and that's about as healthy as our kids' coping skill of using drugs.

We have to stop worrying about other people's triggers and recognize our own triggers and take responsibility for them. No one is responsible for triggering us. We own the responsibility for how we respond to the world around us. And regarding other people's triggers, if we behave rationally and someone else has an irrational response to it, that's not our responsibility. How we respond to their irrational response is our issue.

WHAT WE NEED TO LEARN
TO START DOING

"We can show compassion without taking responsibility."

As parents of addicts, and citizens of the world, we have to learn healthy ways of interacting with people. In this section we'll go over some basic principles and how they relate to our children, and in the next section of the book we'll talk about how we can apply them in all aspects of our lives.

Remember the reality: our child is an addict. They will lie and try to manipulate us out of desperation. They will get angry and behave badly when they don't get what they want. We should expect this and be prepared for it. We need to discover when we should and should not engage and when we do engage, we need to develop the skills to do so in a healthier manner. We need to learn what detachment really means and how to do it lovingly. We need to learn what healthy boundaries look like. Then we need to learn how to set them and hold them even when challenged. All of these things really come down to a form of emotional well-being where we are protecting our own peace and serenity. Practicing healthy interactions means we will no longer relinquish control over our lives to an unappreciative recipient. It's worth noting that when we give up control of our lives and give up all our joy by trying to fix and control everything, no one is actually benefiting. It's not like we are giving our joy to our child. We aren't giving our power and joy away. We are throwing it away. Allowing our child's disease to control our lives isn't helping our child. Giving up our happiness isn't making someone else happy. It's not like giving half your dinner to a hungry person so you can both eat. It's more like throwing your meal onto the floor when you're starving. It serves no purpose and is just an utterly exhausting waste. I often ask parents what brings them joy and they have a really hard time answering. Joy hasn't even been on their radar for so long. Crisis and chaos have become the defining characteristics of their lives. If that's the case with you, that has to change.

Even as parents of addicted kids, we deserve joy in our lives. We deserve to enjoy our lives. We deserve to be happy. We have the right to be happy. We can be sad about our child *and* happy about other things. Chaos and crisis make us see things in extremes; everything is black or white. Studies show how people's ability to make sound judgments is impaired under stress. Stress changes our hormone balance and creates neural pathways that cloud our judgment. When our child is suffering, we find it hard to imagine that it is possible for us to be okay if they're not. We lose sight of the choices we have before us and react in extremes. When we start controlling how we respond to the chaos created by our addicted child, we start to control our lives again.

LEARN HOW TO DETACH FROM UNHEALTHY ATTACHMENTS

> *"We've attached ourselves to our children's emotions and now we have to untether ourselves from them."*

In my experience, detachment is one of the most difficult things for parents to understand and practice. Honestly, I've struggled trying to explain it coherently and effectively in this book. I find that we get caught up in the word instead of understanding how to apply it. In order to understand how to detach, we first have to look at the attachment. Without realizing it, when dealing with our kids and their disease, we have likely become attached to them in unhealthy ways. As described earlier, codependency, enmeshment, enabling, and controlling are all ways that we have become unhealthily attached to our child, emotionally. These unhealthy attachments serve as an anchor keeping us and our child stuck in a bad place. So how do we undo an unhealthy attachment? By detaching. It's that simple. It's not that easy, but it's that simple. The ship can't sail until the anchor is lifted and detached from the sea floor.

Detachment is an emotional practice and when we are learning a new practice, we have to allow for a learning curve. We need to see how a tool works before we can get good at using it. We don't detach from a person; we detach from other people's emotions and problems. Simply put, it's just another way of describing letting go of stuff that doesn't belong to you. It's about our inner emotions, not our outward behavior. If detachment sounds harsh, think of yourself as being untethered. When we untether something, we release it and offer it freedom. We untether a horse so that it can gallop. We untether a boat so that it can sail. We untether ourselves so that we can move forward.

It's not uncommon for me to hear parents say, "I know I have to detach with love, whatever that means," with an eye roll. It is a concept people do not like to consider. They say you can detach with an ax or you can detach with love. Aside from it being very black or white thinking, all or none, my problem with offering these choices is it makes detachment about how you relate to someone else, and that's not what detachment is. You either cut them out of your life, as with an ax, or you love them, and what? When I explain detachment, I'm talking about detaching our own emotions from someone else's emotions, not ourselves from someone else. How we relate to someone else and whether we keep them in our lives or not is a matter of boundaries, not detachment.

Some parents who can't stand their child anymore, for whom life has become a living hell, still can't kick them out but find a way to be at peace in their homes because they have learned how to protect themselves from taking on their child's emotions. And there are parents who do kick the kid out but are still emotionally glued to them. Their separation from their child has not brought them any peace. Detachment is not about physical presence or separation. It's not about supporting them or not supporting them. You can detach whether your child is present in your life or not. Detachment is not removing your child from your life and ceasing to care about them. It's not removing emotion. It's removing unhealthy attachments to other people's emotions. When we talk about detachment regarding our addicted child, we are talking about detaching from the emotional effects that their suffering and disease are having on them. We know that they are suffering but we don't allow their suffering to become our own. We have our own suffering to deal with. And truthfully, if we start putting into practice the behavioral changes that we've already discussed, then we have started to practice detachment already.

We have talked about the need to distinguish our child from their disease. When we untether ourselves from their emotions, we maintain compassion for our child without taking on their pain and misery. We untether ourselves from the effects their disease is having on them so that we can address the effects it's having on us. Detachment is about self-preservation. It's not punitive. We are recognizing and accepting the limitations of our own control over the situation.

I'm writing this book through the covid-19 pandemic. Just think of the precautions we took to protect ourselves or our kids from people with covid. If our kid was positive, we didn't feel guilty about wearing a mask around them or avoiding them as much as we could. We'd bring them food but leave it at the door. This is no different. We didn't want to get covid and we don't want to feel sick like a drug addict when we aren't one. We could care for our kid with covid while protecting ourselves as best we could. We had no trouble not attaching ourselves to their symptoms. We have to learn to do the same here. We have to learn to love them without allowing them to make us sick along with them. Their sadness and loneliness are all symptoms and we can't mitigate those symptoms. We can't cure the loneliness their drug use causes them and when we try, we just become tethered.

All the things we've talked about regarding anticipating their behaviors and avoiding conflict are all ways of detaching. We learn that we don't have to carry their emotional baggage. We don't have to feel their feels. We use detachment to end our enmeshment with our child. We use detachment to stop the cycle of codependency with our child. We have enough of our own stuff to worry about. The more time we spend on other people's stuff the more we just avoid dealing with our own stuff. It's often easier to talk about someone else's mess than to clean up our own. When we practice distancing ourselves from other people's problems, we leave space for us to address our own. Anytime we step into our own power and exert control over our own behaviors, we are detaching from everything else.

I remember a time my son called me from rehab. He had been doing well and he called to talk to me about something that had happened. I don't remember the details, but I remember the emotions. He was upset and I was triggered by him being upset, and I was fighting the urge to succumb to my fear that whatever it was would make him relapse. I thought of all the tools in my new and growing toolbox. I acknowledged that this must be hard. Then I said, "Maybe you could run it by your sponsor." My son replied that he had called his sponsor first! That was when I realized that

I could let go. I could untether myself from his emotions. I could have a good day even if he was having a rough one.

In my practice with clients, I often see that parents have lost confidence in their own parenting skills. After trying to fix their child and failing, through no fault of their own, they lose faith in themselves. As I help them regain their confidence by starting to control the things they actually can, I also help them remember how much they really do love their kids and to develop compassion for their kids. What made it possible for me to be okay even when my son wasn't was that I developed confidence that I wasn't shirking my responsibilities by not trying to fix his problems and I knew, without a shadow of a doubt, how much I loved him. In the throes of his use, all the anger and resentment and fear had clouded that. When I help my clients step back into their power and renew their faith in themselves, coupled with an unclouded love for their child, they become able to see which attachments are unhealthy, untether themselves, and have the freedom to grow.

As we think of unhealthy attachments, we have to look beyond our attachments to people's emotions and look also at our attachments to expectations of the world at large. We have to learn to detach from outcomes as well. We can hope our child gets clean but not live tied to that outcome, because if they don't get clean, then what? We can hope for it, but we have to live whether it happens or not. Detaching from outcomes is reliant on, if not a byproduct of, radical acceptance. We know we cannot control anything in life beyond our own behaviors, so the best we can do is to do our best and let go of the results. The chips will fall where they will, and we will have to adjust. This doesn't mean we shouldn't want certain things and that we shouldn't dream and set goals. It just means that we accept that we can only do what we can do. Once we've done all we can to achieve our desired outcome, we detach from the result. We let go. We accept that it may turn out the way we hope, or it may not. Either way, we will be presented with a whole new set of opportunities to choose from. We have to be careful about what we wish for. We don't always know what's best. All we can do is our best.

When my client's son relapsed for the third time, he was devastated. It turned out that the third time was the charm and after that relapse, his son had had enough and finally embraced recovery. I've met so many men who say going to jail saved them. *Going to jail.* One of a parent's worst nightmares was actually a saving grace. We don't know. We never know. We can spend all our time worrying about our addict dying when any of us can get hit by a car tomorrow. When we learn to detach from the outcome, we allow ourselves to enjoy the satisfaction of doing our best and spare ourselves the worry of *what if.*

When we've been operating around unhealthy and intense attachments for so long, it may be hard to imagine letting go. There's that story about how they used to train elephants. They would tether a baby elephant's front leg with a light rope staked into the ground. The baby elephant would try to pull its foot away but couldn't and would eventually give up trying. As the elephant got bigger and stronger, the trainers never had to change the thickness of the rope, even though the grown elephant certainly could have freed itself from it, because the elephant never realized that it could free itself. It didn't understand that its own strength had grown.

Trust me; you are stronger than you think. We are faced with terrifying situations and even more terrifying possibilities. This is really hard. We're so battle-worn that sometimes we just want to wave the white flag. It's okay. I promise you it can get better. You can get better. Trust me; I've been there. I've been in a place of utter despair, watching my child spiral out of control and I've been left feeling despondent. Then I made the bold decision that this was an unacceptable way for *me* to live and I would seek out any resource to get my own life back. I went to meetings, I read books, I changed the way I acted, I changed the way I thought, and I ended up with a life beyond my dreams. You can get your life back. You can have a better life than you ever imagined. You have to decide you want to and then take actions to actually do it. Get support. Find people who have done it and do what they did to get it. The guidelines in this book show how I did it and how I help other parents do it. These are tools that will help you, but like with any tool, you must hone your skills to use them best. Be patient with yourself but be vigilant and have faith in yourself, and believe that you can make your life better.

LEARN HOW TO NOT ENGAGE

> *"Just because you got an invitation to join an*
> *argument doesn't mean you have to accept."*

I've already talked about superpowers; now I'll offer some magic in the form of phrases that I've learned along the way. Do not underestimate their power to mitigate a potentially volatile situation and do not underestimate their ability to help you reclaim your own power. The beauty of these simple phrases is that not only are they truthful, but they also leave little room for rebuttal, and they actually result in you becoming a better listener because they allow you to simply acknowledge the other person's feelings and struggles without trying to solve their problems, offer them unsolicited advice, or fix them. By using these phrases, we actually make it about them instead of about us.

MAGIC PHRASES:

I'm sorry you're having a bad day.
I'm so sorry you're going through this.
I know it must be so hard.
I'm sure you'll figure it out.
I'm sorry you're having a hard day.
I love you but I have to go now.
Let me think about that.
What's your plan?

Learning to use these phrases literally improved every relationship in my life. Where my son was concerned, using them enabled me to avoid getting sucked into unproductive conversations where he wanted to be antagonistic because that's what addicts do. He would call from rehab and tell me how it sucked. I learned not to say, "Well, you should do this or you should do that." First of all, I didn't work at a rehab so I didn't really know what he should be doing. Plus, he didn't want to hear it from me. How often have you offered your child advice in a similar situation only to have them blow up at you and, of course, ignore the advice anyway? I learned to say, "I know it's hard" or "I'm so sorry you're struggling." At first, I felt like it was so rote and almost insincere but then I realized that it was the truth. I was really sorry that he was struggling, and I knew that it was really hard. Rehab sucks. No one likes it. And as unhappy as he was, he was surrounded by a lot of other people who were just as unhappy and struggling just as much. It gets better, but it's never enjoyable. Some moments are better than others, and if they do the work, they come out better than they went in, but it's not a vacation.

"I love you, but I have to go now" is a great way to bow out of a conversation going nowhere or one that you may find triggering. I'm not talking about a hostile conversation. That can be handled differently. I'm talking about a conversation where the other person is droning on about a lot of crap or when you begin to realize that the conversation is ruining your own mood. Like when your sister is complaining about your other sister and it's the same complaints you've heard for years. No explanation needed. You simply have to go. I can't tell you how often I hear stories from parents about a horrible phone conversation they had. I always remind them that every phone has a disconnect button. Use it. Don't use it without warning, but saying that you have to go is totally acceptable. Remember, you have power in your own life. You can assume control over your interactions. No one gets to decide for you how you spend your time. You don't have to stay in an unpleasant conversation.

I had a client who was very enmeshed with her daughter, and her daughter would call every day and give her every detail of her day. My client was doing a lot of work focusing on her own behavior and becoming un-enmeshed with her daughter. She didn't want to hear every detail of her daughter's life and she also saw the need for both her and her daughter to start expanding their own support circles. She didn't want to be the only one her daughter sought for support. My client started saying, "Sorry, love you, but I have to go," when the conversation got tedious. To her amazement, her daughter didn't really react. They hung up amicably. Eventually her daughter lightened up on the details and they were able to have real conversations about interesting topics and not just tallying the minutiae of everyday life.

My younger daughter is a bold and brilliant woman, and she tends to complain. It always drove me crazy. As I started to look at how I behaved, I realized that I had never been able to show up for her the way she needed me to. My baseline is happy, and I rarely complain. When she complained, from the time she was little, I would always try to fix it. I would offer advice on how to fix it or how to not feel that way. I never knew how to just validate her feelings and I realized that I never let the poor kid just vent without trying to fix it. She was twenty-five years old when I had this revelation. I made my amends and apologized. I told her that I was truly sorry for not being there the way she needed me and that I would do better from that point forward. I started letting her vent and saying things like, "I'm sorry your day sucked," and when I did, I noticed something. Instead of the conversation deteriorating into her being mad at me and both of us feeling like crap, she'd say her piece, I'd say that sucks, and then she'd say something like, "Okay, I gotta go now." Just like that—conversation over and no blood spilled. Go figure. I will never forget the evening when she called me and, for the first time in her life, uttered the phrase, "I need your advice on something." Twenty-five years of unsolicited advice, and when I finally shut up, she actually asked for it.

"I'm sure you'll figure it out" carries a lot of power also. It does two things. First, it tells them that you're not jumping in to fix whatever they need to figure out. How to get gas money, how to pay their phone bill. It doesn't matter. Acknowledging that you expect them to figure it out means you are not taking responsibility for it. It's not your business and it's not your problem. Second, it says that you have confidence that they can handle it. You may have no confidence in the world that their phone won't get shut off, but by saying it, you are planting the seed that they can actually figure it out. Remember, they're resourceful. If they want it, they'll find a way. One client told me that she utters this phrase through gritted teeth because she still wants to jump in and tell them what to do because she has, of course, already figured it out for them. It's becoming much easier for her, but it's hard work.

"Let me think about that" is another brilliant way to give yourself time to think about your answer. Remember, your power lives in the space between the question and your answer, your trigger, and your response. I find that we often overestimate the sense of urgency that our child is working with when we are operating in crisis mode ourselves. Many times they're throwing spaghetti at the wall to see what sticks; in other words, they're tossing out lots of feelers to see what they can actually get from us or get us to do. One of my client's daughters called from rehab with this grand plan for what she was going to do when she got out. It involved her mother's financial assistance and sent the mother's heart racing, but she was doing her own recovery work and learning. She told her daughter she would think about it and let it go. Her daughter never brought it up again. It was a non-issue but engaging in a conversation about it at the time probably would have resulted in the mother saying no to a hypothetical request, and the daughter getting pissed that the mother said no, leading to a confrontation. By saying, "Let me think about it," they went on to have a pleasant conversation that didn't end in a fight and it never even had to be revisited.

Asking your child what their plan is when they are discussing an action they want to take is a great way to put the ball back in their court. If they say they want to do something and that something seems like your involvement may be expected, ask them what their plan is. "I want to leave rehab." Well, what's your plan? It doesn't put you in a position to judge them or offer help. It simply allows them to realize that you are expecting them to figure this out and you are not jumping in to make it happen.

Even if your child is in early recovery, the idea that you have confidence in them can be critical. Addiction whittles away at their self-esteem and confidence. It causes tremendous shame and guilt to surface once they stop numbing it with drugs and alcohol. When we jump in to fix something, we imply that we don't think they can do it without our help. Part of recovery is learning that they can take care of themselves and that they can fix their messes and deal with challenges that come their way without using drugs. When we reinforce this idea and tell them we think they can do it, we're sending a very positive message.

When my son's rehab told me not to pay his rent when he finished treatment, I didn't. In some ways this was a relief of financial burden because I had taken on loads of debt to fund his recovery program and didn't have the money to support an additional household. Still, my son was only twenty years old and working part-time at a bookstore. I was plagued with guilt for not being financially sound enough to support him, even though I was told not to, and afraid of him not being able to make it on his own and afraid of a financial burden causing a relapse. I also just felt bad for him and wanted to help. When I would visit my other kids at college, I would take them grocery shopping and spend some money on them. Here I was being told I couldn't do that for my most vulnerable child. It was really hard for me, but I had committed to doing what I was told. I was giving him the opportunity to prove to himself that he could manage his life without drugs and alcohol. I believed he could do it and I was giving him the chance to believe in himself as well.

When my client's son came home for a visit and announced he wasn't going back to his sober house, my client called me, and I said to ask his son what his plan was. My client did, allowing the two of them to have a real conversation about next steps. The wording showed his son that he was going to have to come up with a plan. Dad wasn't going to jump in here and just say okay. That being said, it also didn't mean that his father wasn't going to help him come up with a plan. The point is, making a decision is not a plan. A decision requires a plan.

Our words are very powerful. A simple turn of phrase can build a person up or knock them down hard. When dealing with our addicted child, the less said is usually best. The predictability of their behavior allows us to anticipate situations we may face and arm ourselves appropriately. In this case, we are not arming ourselves for battle but rather avoiding battle. We are speaking truths without elaboration and acknowledging their emotional needs as well as our own. Use these phrases as they are or make them your own, but remember that their beauty lies in their simplicity. Don't overcomplicate them. Write them down. Put them on your fridge. Jot them on your hand. Take a picture of them with your phone so you always have them. They are power tools to make life easier. Use them.

PICK YOUR BATTLES WISELY

"You can't win them all."

No matter where we are in life, at home, at work, or in a conversation, we need to pick our battles wisely. Setting boundaries can feel like going to battle. You may feel like you are bringing on confrontation, and most of us want to avoid confrontation. For those who like confrontation, we may need to step back and make sure we don't approach our boundaries ready for battle. Confrontation often becomes a way of life when dealing with an addicted kid. We have choices and we can choose our battles. Take an honest look at the last five fights you've had with your addict. Who really started them? When I look at my own experiences and the experiences of the hundreds of parent stories I've heard, often it's actually us. The addict is just doing her thing. She's in her room or in her home thinking about herself and where she's going to get drugs or how she's going to hide the fact that she's an addict. We as parents often insert ourselves unnecessarily.

If your kid doesn't live with you and isn't asking you for rent, why would you ask them if they paid their rent? It's none of your business. Even if they ask you for help, it's still none of your business why they didn't unless you intend to pay it. Don't ask them why they don't have the money. You know why. Don't tell them what they should be doing. They know and they can't. Don't give them money for the rent if they blew their money on drugs.

They tend to be resourceful, and if not, they'll suffer the consequences of their own actions like everyone else. How many times can you think of where you tried to give advice or solve a problem for them, and it turned into a fight?

Addicts can't show up for life the way we hope they will. Their rooms will be a mess, they'll miss deadlines, they'll miss school and work. Managing our expectations can allow us to choose which battles are worth fighting. If your child is going down a rabbit hole of drug use, you may consider saving the energy you use on trying to get them to clean their room and reserving it for the bigger, perhaps more important battle of cutting off their money or taking their car away. As Al-Anon slogans advise, ask yourself:

- How important is it?

- Does it have to be said?

- Does it have to be said now?

- Does it have to be said by me?

- Do I want to be right, or do I want to be happy?

Taking a moment to pause and answer these questions can save a lot of unnecessary battles and a lot of wasted energy that will most certainly lead to frustration and anger.

If your child is in early recovery, this holds true as well. Remember, there is more going on than just use. Your child has a multi-faceted, chronic disease that does not have a cure but will require chronic treatment. Rome wasn't built in a day, and your addict won't be all better after one day, twenty-eight days, or ninety days. That's not how it works. When your child is in early recovery, they are in a battle for their lives, every moment of every day. If they continue to smoke cigarettes or vape but have stopped drinking and doing drugs, pick your battle. If your daughter finally gets clean and dyes her hair red, pick your battle.

If they get a tattoo, pick your battle. Remember, it's not about how you want your child to behave, look like, or be. It's none of your business. You can't have it all. We have to love our children as they are, where they are. That doesn't mean we have to like it, it just means that we must radically accept it. But even more, if we look deep into what we really want for our child, it usually comes down to feelings. We may say that we want our kids to be happy. Happy is an emotion and emotions come and go. No one is happy all the time. What we want is for our kids to have a good life. We want them to be able to handle their lives, be productive, and have meaning in their lives. Most of us don't raise our kids thinking we want them to be a drug counselor, yet many people who go into recovery do just that. A career that was never on our radar for our kids can end up bringing the most joy and meaning to their lives, far beyond our expectations. We don't know what we don't know. Let's focus on ourselves and make sure that we are doing what we are supposed to do for ourselves and let our kids do the same. If our number one hope is that our kids are clean and sober, concentrate on that and celebrate that one day at a time. If they get sober and find recovery, everything else will work itself out, red hair and tattoos or not. If they don't stay sober, nothing will work out. Either way, we need to make sure that we aren't inviting them into arguments, and we need to make sure to say no to their invitations when we can.

ESTABLISH BOUNDARIES

"Boundaries are not about controlling someone else's behavior; they are about protecting our own peace."

Everything we've discussed leading up to now comes down to one of the most important skills we can master in life: establishing and managing our boundaries. Boundaries are a necessary part of every relationship and interaction we have. Boundaries, boundaries, boundaries—one of the most overused and least understood words I know. Boundaries are not rules. They are not a do-and-don't list for other people. Boundaries are not about other people. They are about us. They are about us controlling how we allow the world to impact our lives. We do not set boundaries to change other people or to control situations. We set boundaries to create safety in our own lives and to protect our own peace. When we set healthy boundaries, we take back control of our lives and step into our own power. We tell the world, "You do what you want, and this is the degree to which I *will* participate." Not "I can participate" or "am willing" to participate. Boundaries must be declarative. *I will. I will not.* There is no room for ambiguity. And often, we have to fake it until we make it.

I faked it a lot, and having permission to fake it can give us the freedom to try out our boundaries. Knowing that I could fake it took the pressure off me to try to "get it right." It's impossible to get it right. All we can do is try our best and if our best is to fake it until we make it, then that's what we do. It's a matter of trusting in the process and possibilities.

Here's an example of me faking it. When my son checked himself out of rehab on day three, I told him he couldn't come home. I would not allow him back in my house. That's what his case manager told me to tell him, so I did. I also looked at my twenty-two-year-old son who had just graduated from college and had come home to the hell of living with his addict brother and I thought, *I love Patrick, but I don't love him more than Anthony. How could I tell Anthony I'm letting Patrick come home? We just got rid of him!* Patrick had made our home life hell and at that point, no one wanted him home. We wanted him someplace where he could get help.

Having the support of the case manager and the presence of my older son at home made it easier to utter, "You can't come home," but I had no idea what I really meant by it other than I wasn't buying him a bus ticket, and it was incredibly painful to utter it. I wasn't aware that saying this was just one step of a much bigger process at work, one that I was going into with absolutely no idea of what to expect. My point is I was faking it. I had no idea what I was doing or the implications of what I was doing. I didn't realize at the time that I was setting my first boundary. I had done as I was told. I had surrendered to the expert. But he was my baby and part of me felt like that person who kicks their kid out to be homeless. I wasn't ready for that. The hours he spent wandering around without his phone, which they instructed me not to release to him, were some of the longest hours of my life. I was a wreck. I decided that if he didn't go back to rehab, I'd pick him up and drive west, the opposite direction of home. No real plan in mind other than not to bring him home, but I wasn't ready to allow him to be homeless. My son will tell you that me saying he couldn't come home was pivotal for him. He was left to feel like he had nowhere to go but back to rehab.

I tell you this story because when this happened, I didn't know about boundaries as I do now. I was faking it. I had made the decision to do everything the rehab told me to do so I told him he couldn't come home. If nothing else, it bought me some time to think and time to think is crucial when dealing with the chaos of addiction. That was my first experience setting a boundary and sticking to it, or at least speaking the boundary, not even being sure of what sticking to it would actually look like. I didn't want him home. I wanted him better. I wanted to do everything I could to fix him and help him. I wanted the misery to stop. We were all dying with him in the house. It was hell watching him destroy himself. He was becoming increasingly unpleasant, and I clearly couldn't help him. Having him at home wasn't serving anyone but rather it was destroying everyone. Seeing that first spoken boundary work made me realize I needed to do a lot more of this.

First, it's important to understand the purpose of a boundary. We can't find a solution if we don't understand the real problem. A boundary has been described as something that defines a limit or extent. When dealing with our addicted child, it's important that we determine our own limits of acceptability and the extent to which we will compromise the quality of our own lives. Boundaries are about us. We have already established that we cannot control the addict. We don't set boundaries to control their behavior. We do set boundaries to control the impact that we allow their behavior to have on our lives. Notice "that we allow." We can choose not to allow it. That's what a boundary is, it's us choosing for ourselves.

Second, it's important to understand the anatomy of a boundary. A boundary has to be relevant to the outcome you want regarding your limits. A boundary has to be clear and enforceable and there must be enforceable consequences for violating the boundary. A healthy boundary that we can learn to set, for example, is saying no when we are asked to do something that we don't want to do or that makes us feel uncomfortable. When we say *yes* when we really don't want to, we often end up feeling exhausted, resentful, and victimized. Whether it's that friend or relative that always needs our help or the social or work events that we simply don't want to attend, we have the power to say no. We also have the power to say no without an explanation. We can say it kindly, and we can say it firmly. Boundaries allow us to have relationships where we do not resent the other person. We are in charge of our boundaries and we are responsible for how we respond if someone violates our boundaries. If someone relies too heavily on us for things that they should be managing themselves, we are responsible for saying no and protecting our boundaries. If someone is speaking to us in a way that is unacceptable to us, we have the power and obligation to remove ourselves from that conversation or situation. We can state that we will not tolerate being spoken to like that and if they continue, we can leave the conversation. Boundaries are the way we show respect to ourselves, they are how we honor our own self-respect.

Looking back at how unpleasant our child can become when they are using, we need to apply healthy boundaries that protect us from being subjected to abuse. Abuse can take many forms. It can be verbal abuse; in extreme cases, it can be physical abuse, stealing, or creating an unsafe environment by bringing dangerous people into our homes. I've had many clients whose kids dealt drugs out of their homes or had drugs shipped to their homes. One of my clients was struggling at work. She had a high-pressure, client-facing job and was afraid she would lose it because she found it so hard to concentrate at work. Her daughter was calling her incessantly at work to demand money and tell her what a horrible mother she was. She asked me if it was okay for her not to answer the calls. Of course it was! It's like holding your hand on a hot pan and asking permission to remove it. For so long she had been in this dance with her daughter where she allowed her daughter to sweep her right into the chaos of her addiction that it hadn't occurred to her not to answer the phone until we started talking about it. She hadn't even seen that as a possibility. Yes, parents can practice self-preservation and refuse to answer a call, no matter who it is or how upset they are. This can be really hard. So often we still hold onto the fear that something terrible will happen if we don't answer and the hope that whatever we say will finally be heard. When we can accept how little power we actually have over their addiction, not answering the phone becomes a lot easier.

Diana Clarke, a renowned therapist in addiction, says boundaries are like garden gates; they can open and close depending on the other person's behavior. The ability to end a phone call is a prime example of a super accessible boundary many parents feel the need to ask permission to use. Think of the disconnect button on your phone as a garden gate and feel free to close it to keep out what you don't want in. If you are on the phone with your child and the conversation becomes hostile, I offer you some additional magic phrases. "I will not tolerate you speaking to me like this. If you cannot be cordial, I will hang up." If they continue to be hostile or argumentative, then say, "Okay, I'm going to hang up now." Then actually hang up. Slamming down the phone or hitting disconnect out of anger doesn't serve anyone. When you approach it with a clear boundary, you are disconnecting the call from a position of power over your own life. Remember, that's the goal here: to reclaim our own power. We need to stop letting the addict control how we feel and behave.

Understand, you may scream or cry once you hang up, and that's okay because they won't see that. Your child will sense, perhaps even before you do, that there is a shift in the dynamic. For the first time, they didn't get what they wanted. Once you get through the initial anguish of doing it, you realize that you took the first step to stopping the cycle and taking care of yourself. That's huge.

It can be torturous at first. Feeling like we did the right thing doesn't always feel good. It's unfamiliar and it's scary, but if we keep it up, it starts to feel better. We start to pick up on the sense of relief we have that we didn't get caught in the same old quagmire. It's important for us to slow down and think. All our power lies in the time between the stimulus and our response to it. That's the time when we get to look at our choices before deciding how to respond. We don't slam down the phone. There is no crisis. We give a warning and then hang up. If we operate as if everything is a crisis, we exaggerate the possible repercussions. We have no power over our child's addiction. Our enforcing healthy boundaries will not cause anything bad to happen to them. If something bad happens, it was caused by their addiction. What it will do is allow us to create a life where we have peace and joy, where we can have compassion for our loved ones without taking responsibility.

To determine where we need boundaries, we have to look at what we want to get rid of in our lives. In the depth of chaos, it's hard to see what we want, but it's clear to see what we don't want. Let's start there. Early in my coaching sessions, I often have my clients list out all the things that are driving them crazy or making them miserable. It's easy to feel like your entire life has gone to hell. Actually writing out individual examples of behaviors and situations can help you feel like you are starting to get a handle on it. It's an action step, and any action step we take toward clarity will help empower us. Ruminating over how bad life is, is not an action step. When we write down a list of things that we don't want anymore, it allows us to analyze it, sort it, and prioritize what we can address first.

For my clients Judy and Roger, their son no longer lived at home but constantly asked for money. Money for gas, money for groceries, money for dog food. It's hard for a parent to say no to those kinds of essentials, even though he needed them because all of his own money went to drugs. Judy and Roger made their list and identified asking for money as one of the top things that bothered them. So that's where we started. They used to take him grocery shopping and buy him whatever he wanted. When they got home, they felt resentful and used, understandably so. But even justified resentment is resentment all the same and it's disempowering.

We talked a lot about options. The parents were not at a point where they could say an absolute no, which was okay. I meet clients where they are without judgment and move forward from there. We talked about a small step they could take to change the way they helped their son. They acknowledged that they were helping him so that they "could sleep at night," even though they were getting little peaceful sleep. I helped them realize that they were relinquishing all of their power to their son, and I helped them see that they could continue to help him if they wanted to, but they could do it on their terms, not his. Instead of taking him grocery shopping and giving him carte blanche, they decided they would get a limited supermarket gift card so he could pick up the essentials. They also arranged for dog food to be delivered to his apartment. This gave them some peace of mind that they weren't letting him or his dog starve without creating a situation where they would become resentful. Resentments often form when we feel stripped of power over our lives because someone else is making decisions for us.

We also talked about an exit strategy for their visits with him. We decided that if the conversation went in a direction that the father didn't feel comfortable with, he would simply say that he had to leave. Depending on the situation, he could say, "I won't stay if that tone continues" and if it continued, "I love you but I'm leaving now." Or if the son asked for something else, the father could say, "Let me think about it. I have to go now." When the father brought him the store card, he said it was all they were willing to do. Not all they *could* do but all that they were *willing* to do. The father and son had lunch and a relatively pleasant conversation. The father left without any kind of confrontation. When recounting the story to me later, the father said that it was a relief to know that because he had an exit plan, he knew that he could leave if the visit became unpleasant and he felt relief knowing that his son would not starve without feeling like he had been taken advantage of. Boundaries don't always have to be declared as a boundary. They can be set and held simply by changes in our own behavior. In his head, the father knew that if it got unpleasant, he would leave. He set a boundary and although it wasn't violated in the end, he felt more empowered just knowing he had it at his fingertips.

In the past, this same couple would respond to the request with anger and frustration but then they would do whatever their son requested. They would buy him gas and say, "This has to stop." They would take him grocery shopping and say, "This is the last time." They would say it needed to change and make no effort to change it. This is common when we don't realize that we have the power to change it and when we don't know how to set boundaries. We repeat the same reactions to the same triggers. We can't expect different results from the same behaviors without major frustration. There are always options. We always have a choice. Taking their son to the store, buying whatever he wanted, and saying, "No, we will not buy you groceries" are opposite extremes. There are lots of choices in between. Their son knew it was ridiculous to keep asking for groceries. He didn't argue when they agreed to only a small store card. Instead of fighting with him and lecturing him with empty threats, they took an action step, set up a boundary that served themselves, and respected their own limits. Baby steps are really good as long as they're moving you toward empowerment and peace. The best part was they felt good about it. They didn't just say no and stew on it for days. They worked within their predetermined boundaries and moved on. Brilliant!

Whatever you decide your boundaries will look like, remember that you can start with small things and then move on to bigger things, hence the value in the list. Also remember that boundaries need to be firm, and if they are violated, the consequence involves your own behavior, not theirs. You have to protect your boundary by taking action. The consequence of them being belligerent may be that you end the conversation. You may set a boundary that you will not give them money and if they ask, you say no. Setting a boundary doesn't mean they won't try to violate it, it simply guides you to the action you must take if they do.

Chances are that our addicted child needs to adjust just about every aspect of their lives, but our boundaries have to be more about which of their behaviors affect us the most according to the list we made. Even if they are in rehab, we still have to set boundaries. The first time I visited my son in rehab, I was warned that he might get a little confrontational. I was told to tell him I would leave if he continued. He started in and I did. I will never forget the look on his face when I said I was leaving with fifteen minutes left in the visit. It broke my heart. I can only describe it as a look of bewilderment. I got outside and bawled my eyes out, but he learned the immediate consequences of his behavior and the next visit was much smoother. We joke now about how he couldn't believe I had left. I couldn't believe I had left. It was one of the hardest things I had ever done but staying with him and allowing him to act like that wasn't an option if I wanted things to change for me. None of this is easy but it gets easier with practice and it gets easier when you start to realize that you start to feel more in control of your life again.

RULES VERSUS BOUNDARIES

*"It's not wise to violate rules until you learn
how to observe them." —TS Elliot*

Unlike boundaries, rules are set to guide the behavior of other people. Some rules we set as part of parenting, to help teach our children what is and is not acceptable behavior to us or to society as we see society. Other rules are set to protect our property or our peace of mind. *You can't throw balls in the house because I don't want you to break my stuff. You can't use the car because you never put gas in it even though I made it clear that I expect you to return it with a full tank. If you don't do your laundry, it won't get done.* Some rules have predetermined consequences that can be stated, like the gas in the car.

Other rules can be set with the expectation that they will simply
promote a behavior where the rule won't be violated. Most kids
know not to throw balls in the house. They do it a time or two,
get yelled at or punished, and then they don't do it again. Rules
and consequences are a way of showing others how we expect to
be treated and how we define signs of respect. Rules are about
commanding the respect of others.

When we are dealing with our children and their struggles with
substance use, boundaries and rules become even more important because our child's behaviors and cognitive abilities become
compromised. Verbal consequences, like scolding them for throwing a ball, fall on deaf ears as our child becomes hyper focused
on their need to use substances. When they are in the throes of
addiction, logic, as we know it, does not exist. There is one goal,
to do this one thing that is ruining their lives: use drugs. It seems
crazy to us but to them, it is a matter of survival. They feel they
have no control. They really feel that they need to use to survive.
This is why having consequences for unacceptable behavior is so
vital for our kids. They cannot hear our words, but they can feel
the effects of consequences. People seek help for addiction when
the thought of continuing to live the way they are living while
using becomes less desirable than the thought of getting help. We
may see their lives as miserable, but they are using and numbing
that misery. If we allow them to continue to get what they want
without consequences, we allow their addiction to be tolerable.
When we stop allowing them to get what they want, they become
more and more uncomfortable, and that discomfort may lead to
them wanting to get help. The other reason we need to maintain
our boundaries and rules is because often their behaviors become
so intrusive and disrespectful that our own lives become miserable.
It's hard enough to watch our children suffer and it's even worse
when we feel like our own lives are no better than theirs because
our lives start to be run by a drug addict. Our kid's disease starts

to call all the shots. We have to protect ourselves and our own lives through boundaries and rules.

BOUNDARIES AND RULES WHEN THE KIDS ARE STILL HOME

"My house, my rules."

I've often heard parents of minors, or parents who still have the addict at home, compare and despair and say how it's so much harder for them. The degree to which a parent is challenged is less about the details of the situation and more about the parent's ability to manage how they respond. Don't compare yourself to other parents. None of us really know what's going on in anyone else's lives. We don't know what we don't know. Keep the focus on where you can make a difference: on yourself. If you are allowing the addict to use at home, it's important that you become very honest with yourself. Understand why you are allowing it.

I had a wonderful client who was so traumatized by removing her daughter from her house when she was in her early teens that she allowed her to use in her home when she was in her twenties. We worked together so that she could come to terms with the past trauma and build up the emotional strength to once again have to make difficult decisions. She knew what she had to do, and she knew she wasn't ready to do it. In the time she spent getting strong enough to make the tough decision to send her daughter to a residential facility, I helped her come to peace with her daughter being home and using by managing her expectations around her daughter's behavior, and just as importantly, by finding joy in her own life. I helped her rediscover things that filled her soul and she learned to welcome these things back into her life even while her daughter was there.

Most of my clients who have allowed their child to use at home have done so because they weren't ready to make the tough decisions. They knew they weren't helping their child. They also recognized that they themselves were too beaten down to help them. They were depleted, and when we become depleted, we can't help anyone. If we allow our children to use at home, we become complicit in their use. That is the unbridled truth. It's hard to hear and harder to accept but it is what it is. If we don't want to be complicit in their drug or alcohol use then we need to find better ways of running our own lives, setting boundaries, upholding consequences, and making decisions that are in our best interests. We don't know what's best for our addicted child; all we can do is try to do what's best for us. There is no judgment here. We all do our best. I challenge you to work on yourself so your best gets better, and your decision-making skills improve so that you can do what is best for you and be at peace with those decisions.

I don't want to oversimplify decisions around allowing your child to stay at home, and I can't overstress the need to build a support system for yourself. Living with an addict can be hell and it's vital to make sure that you have enough healthy relationships and interactions to balance your life. It can also be a legal challenge. Depending on the state, you may or may not have a choice. In certain states, if your child can establish residency and prove they have been allowed to be in your home for a time, then you cannot easily evict them—something to consider if you are contemplating allowing your addicted adult to come home, even if for a short while. Certain restrictions also may be in place regarding minors. If your child lives in your home and their car is registered to your address, you can be held liable for their accidents. Also, the truth is that many parents can't imagine actually kicking their kids out. For many who couldn't at one point, that changed, and things got so bad that they were able to. My hope for you is that whether they are there with you or out of your house, you can find peace and empowerment in your own life.

How can you have peace if your kid is shooting up in your basement, not showering, and living like a junky? The short answer is it may be really hard to do. The long answer is to take a good hard look at your situation, be completely honest with yourself and apply all the principles we've talked about to your present situation. What might that look like?

Let's look at what Carmen did. When I started working with Carmen, her son had been using at home for almost four years and she was going to work, coming home to all the household responsibilities, and just completely stuck. It was hard for her to even say she was miserable because she was so disempowered that she was almost numb. She was at the point of setting some boundaries and letting him sleep on a park bench when the pandemic hit. There was no way she was going to kick him out then. The pandemic wreaked havoc in the addiction community, as many of you have felt. Certain options just didn't seem viable anymore.

So here she was, stuck with him using in her house. She was not ready to force him into rehab. He was an adult and had already rejected rehab years before. In a case like this, first Carmen had to look at her whole situation and radically accept where she was at that point. If she was truly not at a point where she could kick him out, then what? She was so depleted; she had no fight left but she had to do something. We started with money. If he had no income source other than her giving him money, that basically made her his supplier, not his loving mother. Radical acceptance— yes, if you willingly give your child money that you know they are using to buy drugs, then you are their supplier. That's not a judgment against you; it's a simple fact that you have to radically accept. Separate your child from their disease and look at which one you are actually serving. Money serves their addiction; it feeds their disease. I coached Carmen to say, "I provide food in the house. I will no longer give you any money." By saying this, she was announcing to herself, her child, and to his disease that she was willing to provide food for her child, not drugs or alcohol for his disease. This wasn't easy for Carmen and choosing to say this to your addicted child will probably cause an argument. You can count on it. But I asked Carmen, do you want to be a loving parent or a drug supplier? Tough love is not about being tough on our children. It's about making tough decisions and having tough conversations. So, Carmen stopped giving her son money. She also told everyone else he might ask about her revelation and her hope that they would not give him money. Then she changed all her passwords and hid all her cards to try to prevent him from stealing money from her.

Next, she stopped cooking meals for him. There was food in the house and he was twenty-seven years old. A fifteen-year-old should be able to cook for themselves. I helped her see that even if she wasn't ready to make him leave, she didn't have to wait on him hand and foot. If he can figure out how to get drugs, he can figure out how to make a peanut butter and jelly sandwich. Clearly, he wasn't worried about a healthy diet, so she didn't have to worry about his diet either. Oddly enough, even when she cut off the money, he still managed to get alcohol. She never found out how.

As the world started to reopen, he started to want to leave the house to meet friends and began to ask her for money again. She would often complain that he never left the house, so now he wanted to leave but said he needed money. She said no; by that point, if he wanted money, he needed to get a job. He cursed and yelled and slammed his door. She anticipated this reaction and was prepared to not engage. All these little steps allowed Carmen to not feel like an unpaid servant to her son or to his disease. Her son was still in the house, but she was feeling better. Her despair had only been partially about him. A lot of her despair came from the mess in her own life that she had allowed his disease to cause. Once she started controlling her own behavior, instead of allowing his disease to control it, she did start to feel better. The situation hadn't changed much, but how she responded had.

Setting boundaries when our kids are still at home is crucial to any hope of sanity for ourselves.

If we tell our kids that we will no longer allow them to use drugs or drink in the house and that they are not welcome to come home high and will not be allowed in, and we convince them that we mean it, they will feel less comfortable. We may not know if we would really lock them out, but we may want to try to at least make them think we would. Remember, fake it till you make it. Kids can usually couch surf for a while, but everyone will be even less tolerant of their crap than you are. A few nights of sleeping hard in the park may be enough for some to say, "Hold on, I'm not doing this." Sadly, of course, as we see so often, some will tolerate living in the park or on the corner. Many of our kids have a dual diagnosis of mental health conditions that make it even more challenging for them to deal with addiction, stress, and life in general. This is another reason why there is no right answer; no one can tell anyone what's best for them. It's okay then to do what's best for us.

There are simple solutions, but they are not easy. I don't want to oversimplify a very complicated situation, but I also don't want you to over-complicate what can be some simple solutions. Knowing what to do is good, but if we don't do it, then the knowledge is useless. How often do we not do what we know we should and not do it? Do we eat right? Do we exercise? Do we drink too much? Still, we get frustrated with our addict when he doesn't do what he knows he should, but he has a disease that tells him not to do it! What's our excuse? Again, focus on our own behavior. Make sure we are doing what we know is the right thing for us. Everyone else can worry about themselves.

If you do decide that your child can no longer be in your home, there are ways to mitigate the fallout of kicking them out. There are also a variety of ways to get them out. Some parents of minors literally have them dragged out in the middle of the night, kicking and screaming, and dragged off to wilderness camp or rehab. Some cut off all supplies of cash and comfort and the kid threatens to leave, and the parents call their bluff.

When we support the disease, we allow it to be tolerable. As long as it is tolerable, the addict will not seek help. The less comfortable we allow them to be in their addictive behaviors, the less comfort we offer them. That's it. That's all we can do. We cannot control their disease or their behavior, but we can learn ways to no longer contribute to their comfort. Comfort is a relative term here. No addict is ever comfortable in the normal sense. However, their use is their comfort zone, even though it's a miserable place and the human mind clings to what is familiar so a place that bears such discomfort becomes their comfort zone. It's the same thing for us as parents. The vicious cycle of chaos and disappointment and pain of our child's addiction in our own lives becomes our comfort zone. We gravitate toward this familiar misery.

All of these practices help us to identify where our comfort zone includes things that actually make us miserable, and they empower us, give us permission, and show us that it's safe to step out of our comfort zones. Often our comfort zones are not happy places. They are familiar places. When misery becomes familiar, our comfort zones become dangerous places. With hard work, we come to believe there is actually something more pleasant than our comfort zone. As we stop engaging, learn to detach from the disease, set boundaries, and start focusing on our own lives, things start to work themselves out. Sometimes the addict leaves on their own because staying doesn't serve them to stay any longer. Sometimes we begin to see that it doesn't serve us any longer and we make them leave, but we are able to do so from a place of power rather than desperation. We move from our comfort zone to our empowerment zone.

Many parents hire interventionists to help. The interesting thing with interventionists is that they don't deal with the addict until the actual intervention. They spend most of their time working with all the loved ones involved and making sure that they are on the same page. They have to make sure Grandma won't take him in if Mom and Dad kick him out or that Mom won't take him in if Dad kicks him out. Once they get the loved ones on the same page, they each usually write out how the addict's behavior has affected them, and then during the intervention they read them to the addict. Note that they don't tell the addict what they should do. They tell the addict what their behavior is doing to them. One interventionist said that what often happens is his team will arrive, and the addict will be asleep because that's what addicts do, and he'll go in and wake the kid up and the kid will take one look at the strangers around his bed, who are usually big guys, and say, "Okay, I'll go" before they even have the sit-down with the family. This is because by the time the moment comes, the family has already started behaving differently and the kid has picked up on this. Addicts are smart. They usually know when the gig is up. They may keep trying, but they may become wearier as they do. This is what we hope for, but whether it helps them get help or not, boundaries help us live better in our own lives and that's all we can do.

MANAGE OUR EXPECTATIONS

*"Most of our biggest disappointments are the
result of mismanaged expectations."*

Growing up, I often heard adults say, "Be realistic," and usually it was in response to me dreaming big and them failing to see my dreams the way I did. In the coaching world we identify that as a classic case of instilling limiting beliefs, and I've worked hard to identify and get over many of my own limiting beliefs. I was being discouraged from taking risks of dreaming big and encouraged to stay safe by keeping it small. In the dating world, there was a trend decades ago to associate the problem of finding a partner with standards that were too high, and this was immortalized by *Saturday Night Live* when Jon Lovitz doled out the advice to all single women over thirty to "lower your standards." Managing expectations is not lowering your standards, nor is it being "realistic" in the sense of limiting what you wish for. When we manage our expectations, we are able to stay in charge of our lives while accepting that we are not in control of everything.

Being in charge and being in control are very different. Most of what goes on in our lives is out of our control, particularly the behavior of others. When we control the things we can control, namely how we respond to the world around us, we remain in charge of our lives. We can look at all the choices before us in any given situation and decide how we will respond. When we take back the power that we have relinquished to our child's addiction, we once again, become in charge of our own lives. Managing our expectations in all areas of our lives is an important way to remain in charge of our lives. It not only helps us avoid disappointment and resentment but actually leads us to greater joy.

I consider managing expectations to be a skill that we can acquire, and it's a skill that I teach all the time. For the last few years, I've run a workshop around finding joy during the holidays and a lot of the workshop focuses on managing expectations. I break it down to managing the expectations of others and managing our expectations of ourselves. We need to do both in order to find peace and joy.

With regards to our addicted children, the ability to manage our expectations goes back to radical acceptance, and allows us to meet them where they are rather than where we wish they were because where they are is the only place we can help them.

Our kids are really struggling. When we expect them to show up for life and function in ways that there is no evidence that they will be able to, we end up angry with them, disappointed, and resentful. It's like when we had a newborn. If we expected them to be on a schedule that first month that allowed us to sleep and feel rested, we were in for a rude awakening. People with a newborn should expect to be exhausted for at least a couple of months. Parents with a child struggling with substances should expect that things will not go as the parent planned. If our child barely got out of high school, we shouldn't expect them to be able to handle college. If they got fired from one job, we shouldn't expect them not to get fired again. If nothing changes, we shouldn't expect to see a change. It sounds obvious and logical, but in the chaos of addiction, we often mismanage our expectations. One definition of insanity is doing the same thing over and over and expecting a different result. Until we see meaningful changes in our child's behavior, we should not expect to see meaningful changes in their situation and abilities.

Expectations are fluid. As people and situations change, so too should our expectations. If our child starts to get sober, our expectations can change. We can proceed with cautious optimism in the beginning at least, and as they start showing up more in their own lives, we can adjust our expectations for how they show up in our lives as well. This is another reason why it's so important for us to focus on our own healing and growth. When these positive changes happen, we want to be able to see and feel them rather than be stuck in the old emotions and reactions that we had when they were using.

Managing our expectations for ourselves is also important. When we can stop expecting that we can fix things that are out of our control, we can start to focus on what we can control. It's important that we manage our expectations around our own capabilities and limits. We can't expect people to know what we want or need if we don't know what we want or need.

My client Kate was always furious with her husband for not doing what she wanted him to do and understanding how exhausted she was. Meanwhile she went around all the time like there was nothing wrong and like she could handle it all. It's unrealistic to expect people to read our minds, especially if we are going to great lengths to hide our emotions. We dug deep and I worked with Kate on figuring out what all the things causing her to feel overwhelmed and under-supported were. Then we teased out what she really needed from her husband and found a way to articulate exactly that. She also learned to be more honest about the burden she was carrying. Some of that burden couldn't be shared and just had to be released. Some of it could be shared, and when she began communicating with her husband about her needs, they were able to manage expectations together around their roles in supporting each other. Those managed expectations led to Kate and her husband fighting less and communicating more and helped them get back on the same page when making decisions about their son.

We can't do life alone, especially with a child who is struggling. It's okay to ask for help. It's okay to spend time thinking about what we really need and how those needs might be met. It's unrealistic to think that we can be all things to all people and still maintain our own health and sanity. When we manage expectations around ourselves, we can release so many of our own burdens and give ourselves the grace to not be perfect and not be everything for everyone and to see the value in taking care of ourselves first. It doesn't mean we only take care of ourselves, but that we prioritize ourselves. When we can identify what we really want, we can find joy again.

A personal example of the benefit of digging deep when managing expectations came to light a few years ago on Thanksgiving. My kids would always nap after dinner and I would be left the only one awake and feeling a little lonely. My kids are all adults. They all work full-time and have busy lives and I see them often. I thought about it as Thanksgiving approached and realized that if I felt lonely when they slept, that was my problem to solve, not theirs. Whatever caused me to feel that way was not just their napping. Then I thought about what I really wanted on Thanksgiving. I want to spend all day cooking delicious food that my family will enjoy, and I want to watch my kids being happy to be together. If they wanted to nap, why do I care? If I wanted to nap, I could too; I just don't like to nap. I decided that I would let go of expectations around what everyone did and focus on how the day felt instead. Not having to worry about how everyone was going to behave made me much more relaxed as I cooked. Even those last minutes just before presenting the bird were relaxed. We had normal, jovial banter as we ate, and when we finished, all four of my kids and their significant others piled on my giant sectional sofa with the dogs and took a collective nap. I got what I wanted. All my kids were together and enjoying each other's company, even if it was just shared warmth on the couch. I didn't lower my standards or diminish my dreams. I simply got to the heart of what I really wanted and allowed for that.

When we mismanage our expectations, we fill our mental room with clutter and we don't allow room for what we really want. When we manage our expectations focused on what we want to ultimately feel, and not the details of how everyone is behaving or what exactly we are doing, we put ourselves back in charge. We avoid disappointment and resentment and set ourselves up to feel peace and joy.

THE DRY DRUNK PARENT

"If a drunken horse thief stops drinking, you're just left with a sober horse thief."

The idea that our child not only gets sober *but also* finds recovery is an important concept not to be easily dismissed. Have you ever heard the expression "a dry drunk"? It refers to an alcoholic who has stopped drinking but has not changed any behaviors associated with being an alcoholic. It's not about the person who realized they drank a bottle of wine a night and stopped or the guy who drank at business lunches and dinners and realized it was unhealthy. This term refers to the person who was a full-blown alcoholic with all the associated behaviors of lying, manipulating, and gaslighting, who simply stopped drinking. The person who drank to fill the hole in their soul. They stop drinking, but the hole is still there. Dry drunks tend to be mean and difficult because alcohol was their only coping mechanism, and when that was taken away and not replaced by a program of healthier coping mechanisms, they just get really angry and frustrated because now they have nothing to numb all these feelings, and they are also no better equipped to deal with them. Only true recovery fills the hole.

A parent who has not changed their thoughts and behaviors even when their child's situation has changed is like a dry drunk parent. It's the parent who kicked the kid out and is not any happier or any more at peace than when their child was home. It's the parent whose kid has been sober for three months and still thinks they can go back to college without additional support. Addiction treatment is not a one-and-done. It's a chronic disease and we as parents have to be prepared to treat ourselves chronically as well. One of my favorite anecdotes that I heard early on in my own journey was about a guy who went home to visit his mom, and he was running out for milk and she panicked and asked him where he was going. He said, "Mom, I haven't had a drink in twenty-seven years. Why are you still freaking out?" She said, "It's like yesterday to me!" This made me laugh, as it was intended, but it also made me say, "God, I don't want to be like that." I didn't want to be able to relate to her. I didn't want to be like her. I wasn't supposed to want to be like her; that's the point of the story. What good to us is our kid's sobriety if we live in the same fear we had when they still used? We got what we wished for, and we are no happier. This is exactly why we need to work on ourselves.

When my son was in the early months of his twelve-month residential program, one of the caseworkers relapsed and was dead within three days. It was devastating, even for the parents who didn't know him. It sparked immediate fear about the effect it would have on our kids in early recovery. We were also crushed by the reality that it could happen to anyone at any time. You know it, but until it happens, you're never prepared. One of the mothers said she asked her son how he felt about it and he said, "Mom, I have a fatal disease that will kill me if I don't treat it every day." This is the importance of a program. People in the world of addiction become accustomed to death. It is a fact of life that they are forced to face much more often than the general population. They live in a war zone. Many battles are fought silently and may go unnoticed, and many battles are lost. Programs come in all shapes and sizes. There are twelve steps and modified twelve steps. Some use the gym as a program. Some find it in spirituality through church groups or temples. There are many paths to recovery for our child to take and the goal is to just be on one. They can redirect if they need to, but if they are moving forward, then they are moving in the right direction. The same goes for parents. We have to embark on a journey of recovery and personal growth ourselves so that we do not relapse into our old behaviors and we can remain in our own power, in charge of our own lives.

What I learned most from that experience was that I had a lot of work to do. My son was battling a chronic, potentially fatal disease and I couldn't help him. It was truly out of my hands. All I could do was focus on my own behavior and how I was showing up in my own life. My son's battles were his to fight and my battles were mine. What I also came to realize was that the weapons that could help us were similar. That's why in Al-Anon you work the same twelve steps as in Alcoholics Anonymous. And if you read most philosophers, modern religious teachings, along with ancient Hindi and Buddhist teachings, the messages are all the same. Mind your business. Focus on your own behavior. Own your mistakes. Celebrate your wins. Behave the way you wish others did and treat people the way you want to be treated. Love yourself and know that everything you need to be fulfilled is already inside you. Joy and peace and love come from within. That's why people with "great" lives can still be miserable and people with "miserable" lives can still find joy. When we talk about recovery, we are talking about recovering our own potential to allow ourselves to find peace and joy and meaning in our own lives, no matter what.

What I learned from what I refer to as "working my own program," attending Al-Anon meetings and parent support groups and working on my own personal growth with the help of coaches and other types of growth and leadership programs, has made me a better person in every aspect of my life. I have become a better friend. I listen and I don't give advice. I called many of my friends when I had my ah-ha moment around always knowing what was best for everyone. I don't. I barely know what's right for me. I immediately called my closest girlfriends as I walked home from an Al-Anon meeting and thanked them for still being my friend after years of telling them everything they should do whether they asked or not. I became a better mother. I listen better, I am more patient, and I am more respectful of their individuality and adulthood. In other words, I mind my business and respect their choices. And if I have an opinion that was not invited, I shut my mouth. And when I don't shut my mouth, which happens because it's about progress, not perfection, I try to catch myself, I apologize, and I back off. I have become a better citizen of the world by becoming clearer on what I want my life to look and feel like. My life is no longer defined by addiction nor is it defined by being a mother since my children are now independent adults. I have been able to find purpose outside of motherhood, like writing this book and helping as many people as I can. I have become more brave. I don't have a lot of fear anymore. I trust in the universe in ways I never did before. I can truly let go of results and have a tremendous amount of inner peace. I like to think that I have become what Vishen Lakhiani, in *The Code of the Extraordinary Mind*, calls unfuckwithable.

I used to describe myself as a rock. A hard surface that can get rammed repeatedly and not break. I don't have to be a rock anymore. I don't have to take on everyone else's stuff. I don't have to do everything for everyone without help. I can be compassionate without taking responsibility. I can help people without doing for them and can ask for help without feeling weak. I no longer wear busy and overwhelmed as a badge of honor. I see it as a malady for which there is treatment. The treatment is all the things we've been discussing. The outcome is a peaceful and balanced life where I feel empowered and I choose when to say yes and when to say no. And let me tell you, it's a great place to be.

My program has changed over the years. As parents, we can take many paths. We need to choose one that will lead us to a more peaceful, joyful life filled with meaning and purpose. That's the destination. We get there through self-reflection, self-assessment, and self-improvement. We have to work hard on improving ourselves. When we get better, everyone around us benefits, but that's not why we do it. We do it because it is all we can do. The only thing we can control. If you remember the Superman reference earlier in the book and how his superpower of x-ray vision worked as long as he wasn't looking through lead, our own superpower only works as long as we use it to control ourselves.

I did Al-Anon, and I worked the steps with a few different sponsors. I still facilitate parent support groups. I meditate and defend my morning routine against any interruption. I continue to read something spiritual and personal growth-related every day. I journal every day and set my intentions for the day. I have spiritual and thought leaders that inspire me, and I follow what they write and try to apply what I like to my own life. I work with coaches who help me envision the constant growth of my life and what the next big thing I want to accomplish will be. I remain vigilant about holding myself accountable for my own behavior and course-correct when necessary. Addiction keeps our lives small. My life has expanded exponentially as I worked to recover from the effects of my son's disease. It got me to work on things that needed work even before he got sick. I encourage you also to think big.

Getting help for our child is only part of it, and it's the part we have the least control over. Our lives have room to grow when we allow them to. Think big; where do you want your life to go?

In the next section of this book, we will discuss how to start thinking of your life in terms of you again and how to start making decisions that lead to your own mental and emotional health. How to really focus on your own responses and behaviors. What self-care looks like and why it's so important. We'll talk about morning routines and living with intention. As I said earlier, the universe can't give you what you want if you don't know what you want. Figuring out what brings you joy and lights you up is a good place to start. I can't say that I'm happy that my son suffers from addiction or that I'm happy for all the pain and loss we went through around his addiction and how we all ended up sick. I will say that I am a better and happier person for it. I will say that the struggle resulted in an opportunity for personal growth that I could never have imagined. And I will say that I have seen hundreds of people who can say the same thing. There is so much hope left for each of us as parents of addicts. Embrace the opportunity, learn all you can from it, and use that knowledge to propel you forward into a life you could only dream of. That's what our child is told to do in recovery and that's what we must do as well.

PART II

SHIFTING THE FOCUS OFF OF OUR CHILD AND ONTO OURSELVES

Addiction is a family disease, but recovery is personal.

OUR LIFE IS ABOUT US

"Doing things for our own well-being is never at the expense of someone else's well-being. It may be at the expense of their comfort, but not their well-being."

So far, we've talked a lot about addiction and our child. We talked about the importance of radically accepting that our child has a disease and that that disease is out of our control. We've talked about the nature of the behavior of the addict and how to manage our expectations around their disease. We learned how to separate our children from their disease so that we can make better decisions around them. We've seen things we need to stop doing and things we need to start doing in order to have a healthier relationship with our sick child. We've started to fill a toolbox with tools to help us with our child and their disease. The first sections of this book focused on our relationship with our child and our child's disease.

Now we get to focus on ourselves. We get to look at how we are showing up for ourselves and how we can show up better. We get to understand what I call Soul Care. Self-care is a term that's always thrown at parents. What does that even mean, and how do we even begin? Parents are told to focus on themselves. How can we do that when there is so much going on? We will learn how to identify our own needs as well as how to focus on our own

responses to things that are out of our control and begin taking
responsibility for things that are in our control. We will learn how
to be in charge even when we are not in control. We'll add to our
toolbox and fill it with tools to help us rebuild our own lives. And
we will learn ways to discover joy in our everyday lives by caring
for our souls.

To begin to reclaim our lives, we must first accept and understand that our children's disease has altered our current psychological and emotional state and we have developed unhealthy
behaviors and habits because of it. We have conditioned ourselves
to feel like we have no control over our lives and have developed a series of habits that allow things around us to control
our decisions and our actions. Think of all the times we are left
uncomfortable with the way we have reacted to our child. Did
we give in even when we didn't feel good about it? Did we allow
behavior that we felt was unacceptable? Did we begin to walk on
eggshells so as not to poke the beast? We've stopped acting like
we have any power; therefore, we don't. Even if our child gets
sober, these behaviors and thought patterns don't magically go
away. We have to course-correct our own lives and our own ways
of thinking. The source of our current chaos and misery is not
only our child's addiction but also the way we have responded to
our child's addiction; our own behaviors and thought patterns.
This is not meant to be a statement of blame or criticism. It is a
statement of empowerment. Our reactions are actually something
we can control, so we can decide how to respond to the world,
improving our feeling of control over our lives and our ability to
find peace and joy. Our peace and joy will no longer depend on
our child and their addiction.

I coach a lot of parents who have a very hard time coming
to terms with the role they may have played in their own lives
and that of their child. It becomes easy to blame all of their own
misery on the addict or the disease since the resulting behavior

is objectively unacceptable. It's often hard to accept that the way they themselves have responded to certain situations has contributed to their own misery. On the one hand, they feel a tremendous amount of shame and guilt that their child is an addict. They also feel a tremendous amount of resentment and anger toward their child for the ways they have behaved. When advised to look at themselves and how they have behaved, they get defensive. Their child's behavior is objectively unacceptable—stealing, lying, using drugs—yet I ask the parents to take responsibility for their own part.

Let me make this clear: as parents, we are not responsible for our child's behavior. We are responsible for how we respond to it, and how we respond to it determines our own sense of control and our own peace of mind. Remember, we talked about them having their drug of choice and them becoming our drug of choice. We may not be contributing to our child's behavior, but we are contributing to our own misery when we relinquish control over our response and allow fear, often panic, to make us react.

Think about how your heart reacts when the phone rings. Notice how dry your mouth gets; your stomach and back muscles tighten, and your heart starts to race. Often the sound of our phone ringtone is an incredible emotional and physical trigger. One of the first things I often do with my clients is get them to change their ringtone. This eliminates the physical flight or fight response to the trigger and gives them a moment to respond in a healthier way, like maybe not even answering the phone at that very second. Once we realize that our present state is the result of conditioning and habits we've developed, we are empowered to recondition ourselves and change our habits. We are back in control.

MY LIGHTBULB MOMENT: I WAS A TRAINWRECK

*"I realized that my son getting sober didn't
mean I was suddenly ok."*

When my son went to rehab, I was told to send him to a particular twenty-eight-day program and do everything they told me to do. I did as I was told and promised myself that I would do everything they told me to do and nothing that they told me not to do. Looking back now, I realize that my willingness to give up control early on saved me a lot of distress moving forward. I knew I was out of my depth. I had tried everything I could think of to help my son, and nothing worked, which was obvious because things were getting worse instead of better. There was a huge sense of relief when I handed over the decision-making around my son's disease to the professionals whom I decided to trust. Those professionals ended up recommending a twelve-month program after the twenty-eight-day program ended. I was a little taken aback, but I was slowly gaining an understanding that this was not a one-and-done thing. People don't go to rehab for twenty-eight days and come back cured. I did what I was told and managed to find the money for the program.

That program had a great family program that included a
parent support group and a workshop each month. I would drive
almost two hours from New York City to New Haven, Connecticut
twice a month and attend every meeting and workshop. At the first
workshop I attended, a person from the leadership team shared
his journey of recovery with us. I listened intently, hanging onto
every word. I had never heard a drug addict or alcoholic talk about
their addiction. He talked about his addiction and his relapses
and what happened when he finally found long-term recovery.
He kept talking about "his program" and how at one point, he
had checked himself back into rehab before he had even relapsed
because he knew he wasn't working a strong enough program.
Then he said how important it was for us, as parents, to work our
"own program." I didn't know what a program was at that point,
but it seemed damn important, so sticking to my commitment to
do as I was told, I started attending Al-Anon meetings.

I arrived at my first Al-Anon meeting, following a long day at
work, fifteen minutes before the end of the meeting. People were
talking about the twelve steps and working with their sponsors and
I thought I had entered an AA meeting by mistake. I hadn't known
what to expect and I was confused. Then someone read the closing
statement, which is pretty standard across meetings, and I heard
the line "although you may not like us all, you will come to love
us the same way we already love you," and began to sob my heart
out. After the meeting they sold books, and I bought three daily
readers and a couple of books explaining how Al-Anon works. I
read like crazy that week and learned that in Al-Anon they work
the same twelve steps as in AA and you can work with a sponsor
in Al-Anon just like in AA. The next week I went back, arriving
a little earlier but still not on time. This went on for a couple of
weeks and I kept asking myself, "Why do I need this? Patrick is in
rehab and I'm fine." I'm laughing at the absurdity as I write this.
Around my fifth or sixth meeting, someone did a reading about

behaviors. I don't even remember which reading it was, but I remember feeling like I got hit by a bolt of lightning as I realized that I was not fine, but rather, I was, in fact, a complete train wreck. I had become someone that I didn't recognize and didn't even like. I wasn't the kind of mother I wanted to be to Patrick or my other three kids. My household had become chaotic, and I had no emotional energy for any of my kids. I wasn't the friend I wanted to be because I had basically isolated myself from all my friends. I wasn't a decent sister or aunt. My son's addiction had made me sick, and I had started to behave like I had his disease. He had his drug of choice, and he became my drug of choice and, in an effort to save him, I would treat those around me the same way he did when he needed to use. I would get his siblings to take on his responsibilities. I would violate his privacy and go through his stuff. I would find drugs or alcohol that belonged to him, and I would take it and get rid of it. I became obsessed with him and the only thing I focused on was him. I focused on absolutely everything about him. On the surface it seemed like reasonable behavior and like my intentions were noble, which I do think they were. I was trying to save my son. What I came to realize through working my own program was that however reasonable and noble my behaviors may have seemed, they were clearly misguided and ineffective in saving my son. What they were effective in doing, was making me a trainwreck in my own life.

I came to see that I had allowed the chaos and destruction of addiction to become my normal. I'd created a new normal for my life that wasn't centered on me using drugs but was centered around Patrick's drug use. My life had become as completely derailed as his, and I hadn't even seen it happening. That's what happens when we spend all our energy focused on someone else—we lose focus on our own lives. When we were kids, they used to tell us to never wear someone else's glasses because it would ruin our own eyesight. They were right. And when we focus on the wrong things, like looking through the wrong pair of glasses, we stop being able to see anything clearly and we end up having to relearn how to show up for ourselves, how to take care of ourselves, and how to build a life for ourselves that brings us peace and joy.

As sobering as this initial realization was, it was also a relief and actually got me excited. For the first few months of my son's treatment all I heard was how I couldn't control anything. I appreciated the relief from responsibility, but I also felt powerless from that thought. I can't control it or fix it, so does that mean I'm just a bystander, like the people who can't stop staring at a car crash? Realizing that there were times when I was at fault, where I was contributing, if not to his drug use, certainly to my own misery, I discovered that I actually could control a lot of things and that I did in fact have a tremendous amount of power

Going back to the Superman analogy from earlier, when I used my power to change myself, I could make my life better. I could become the person I wanted to be instead of the person I had become when I started letting my child's disease rule my life. I could become the mother, friend, and sister I wanted to be. I didn't have to give up all control; I just had to stop trying to control things I couldn't and focus on the things I could. After that night, I changed my work schedule so that I would not be late for my meeting again.

Over the course of the next year, I attended Al-Anon meetings, as well as the parent support group and monthly workshop offered by my son's recovery program. I attended open AA meetings with some Al-Anon friends to hear stories and better understand what my son was facing. But more than attending meetings, I made radical changes in how I was showing up in my own life. I took action. I began to strategize my life and my own recovery. First, I built a morning routine focused on healthy thinking and intention setting. I also started shifting my focus from my son's life back to my own life. For example, I started taking care of all the stuff I had stopped taking care of. I went to the doctor and dentist, paid outstanding parking tickets, got my laundry done, and began reaching out to friends again. I started asking how my other kids were instead of just using them as sounding boards for my stress over Patrick. I changed a lot of things, big and small. Information without implementation is a missed opportunity. It's one thing to go to meetings and learn what changes you have to make; it's another thing to actually make those changes.

My clients see success when they work with me because I help them design their action steps and hold them accountable for taking those actions. Knowing what to do and actually doing it are two different things. Knowing what to do isn't enough. You have to actually do it. The key is taking action.

In the next few chapters I will share how to determine your action steps that will lead to a more empowered, peaceful, and joyful life. We'll learn some new habits you can develop to help you break the patterns that lead to misery and chaos. I will show you what I did and what I have helped other parents do to reclaim their power in their own lives, maintain a sense of peace, and find joy in their lives. We need to remember that our peace and joy should not depend on our child. Our child's disease can make us sad, even heartbroken, but it doesn't have to break us. We can be okay even if our child isn't. We can find ways to manage the pain of seeing our child sick so that we no longer allow their disease to control our lives. We can learn to be happy and sad at the same time.

SOUL CARE

*"Take care of your soul as if you were going
to die tomorrow." —St. Augustine*

The kind of practices that lead to long-term changes in thinking
and behavior are what I like to call "Soul Care." They are the
things that tend to our souls, not just to the details of life, but to
our very core. They are things we do to help develop and nurture
the very foundation of who we are and who we want to be. Soul
Care allows us to remember who we are, separate from all the
stuff we've dealt with and all the distractions of our lives. Soul
Care brings us back to who we were before the world got in the
way. It brings us back to who we wanted to be before we were
told it wasn't possible. It helps us rediscover the joys we used to
have and the dreams we used to have and discover new ones. It
helps us discover what really lights us up. When we care for our
souls, we allow ourselves to discover all the potential of our own
lives even if those around us aren't seeing their own potential.

It's not about being happy. Happiness is fleeting. Happiness is
an emotion. Soul Care is about being alive in our own lives. It's
about having dreams and aspirations no matter what stage of life
we're in and no matter what chaos ensues around us. Soul Care
encompasses the practices that make our lives worth living. It's
what gives our lives purpose and meaning and drives us to keep

going no matter how difficult things get. Soul Care builds resil-
ience and fortitude. It helps us identify what we want our lives to
feel like and look like. When we spend time getting to know what
we want in life we become more confident and difficult decisions
become much easier because we trust ourselves more; we feel
empowered. When faced with a difficult decision, we will be able
to determine which choice will allow us to live with integrity and
be true to ourselves. We can move forward with the confidence
and understanding that making decisions in our own best interest
is never at the expense of someone else's well-being. It may be at
the expense of their comfort but not their actual well-being. We
can create a life that's worth protecting, and one of the best ways
to protect it is to stay out of other people's drama. To support
people and to do it in such a way that we are not compromised
and depleted and, that we don't feel disempowered or resentful.
We come to learn that when we help others, we can do it on our
own terms, by choice, and equally importantly, we are able to let
go of the outcomes of the help we give. Letting go of outcomes is
a big part of Soul Care. With regard to helping others, our help is
a gift. What a person does with that gift is none of our business.
We help others in order to be at peace ourselves. This may sound
selfish on the surface but it's not.

Think of all the times you've helped people because you felt
you didn't have a choice. Perhaps it was your child, sibling, parent,
or friend who asked you for help, and somewhere deep or maybe
not so deep, you just didn't want to do it. Not like when you were
a rebellious teenager and your mom said to take out the garbage
and you didn't want to. I'm talking about somewhere deep inside
your gut, you had that feeling that you shouldn't have to do this.
How resentful or disempowered did you feel when you said yes?
With regard to outcomes around things working out the way we
want them to, knowing that we did our best and that that's all we
can do frees us of the worry of how things will work out. We can

let go of the outcome and know that with every situation new choices are presented to us and we will be able to find solutions for ourselves no matter what.

When we practice soul care we can identify, understand, and start to trust that gut feeling. We can also reframe so that even though we may end up doing the same action, our feelings about doing it can change. We can do it in such a way that we feel it is our choice. We can help identify what our motive is, which is often tied to expectations of the result of our help, and we can train ourselves to manage those expectations by letting go of the results. Earlier I mentioned that addicts often refer to the hole in the soul. We as parents of addicts also develop a hole in our souls and Soul Care is how we heal it.

WHAT DOES SOUL CARE LOOK LIKE?

The two main components of Soul Care can be identified by two well-known, albeit often confusing terms: self-care and focusing on ourselves. We hear these terms a lot when we have a child who is struggling. Everyone—professionals, friends, people in support groups, they all tell us to "take care of yourself," to "focus on yourself." But what does that mean and how do we begin when self-care has been off of our own radar for so long?

I also find many parents resisting because they equate these two concepts with being selfish. There is nothing selfish about taking care of yourself, just like there is nothing noble in not taking care of yourself. We see our kids neglecting themselves and we complain, yet we often fall victim to the same self-neglect. We also look at how our kids are responding to the world, and we know that the response is not healthy, yet we don't spend time looking at how we are responding to the world. Self-care and focusing on ourselves are two different things and equally important in order to heal the hole in our souls. One is about caring for ourselves and one is about taking responsibility for how we show up in the world. When we begin to improve both, how we show up in our own lives and how we show up in the world, we begin to heal the hole in our own souls. As our souls heal, peace and joy become more available to us. They've been available to us all along. We just lost focus.

SELF-CARE

"A depleted person can't help anyone."

Self-care comes down to identifying our needs and wants and making sure that they are being met on a regular basis so that we can feel confident and empowered in our lives. There can be physical, emotional, spiritual, and intellectual needs and wants, and if all are not tended to, the hole in our soul will remain open.

Self-care is a misunderstood concept and so many of us fall into the traps of those misconceptions. There's the martyr trap—self-care is selfish. There's the distraction trap—self-care involves keeping really really busy with work or tasks that have nothing to do with making you feel better. There's the appearance trap—I got my hair done and a pedicure but as soon as I get home I felt like crap again. That's "taking care" of yourself but it's not real self-care. There's also the exercise trap—running is not necessarily self-care. To start, there is basic self-care, like hygiene and personal appearance, going to the doctor, eating right, and staying fit, many of which fall by the wayside for us when our kids are in distress. When was the last time you were at the dentist? Things like manicures can be a very basic form of self-care, as can things like walks in nature or a round of golf. They can be pampering and bring us pleasure, but often don't carry long-term effects. The moment we are brought back to the challenging situation or the reality we were taking a break from, all of that momentary peace is gone, and we find ourselves no better equipped to handle reality. Basic self-care can be a big part of maintaining peace and serenity in our lives, but we need more than the basics.

We also need to look at our deep emotional needs. Do we know what we need and want and are we making sure we get it? Are we asking for help? Are we expecting others to know what we need and resenting them when they don't provide it? Do we say yes when we want to say no? Are we setting boundaries that allow us to have the life we want, or are we letting others control our lives? Our emotional needs and the state of our own lives are our responsibility, no one else's, and solid self-care practices allow us to identify what we need and want in our lives and empower us to get it. This leads us to feel better in control of ourselves and more confident so that we can make better decisions and respond better to the world around us.

It's important to understand that taking care of ourselves doesn't mean we stop taking care of others where appropriate. The idea of self-care being selfish goes back to the black and white, one extreme or the other thinking in the midst of chaos. It's not all or nothing, I either take care of myself or I take care of everyone else. A healthy self-care practice means you are making sure your own needs are met so that you are better, and when you are better, everyone around you benefits. If you do have to take care of others, you can do it from a place of strength rather than a place of depletion and exhaustion. Everyone benefits when we are at our best, when we are fulfilled and calm and confident. No one benefits when we are a stressed out and exhausted trainwreck. When the flight attendant instructs us to place the oxygen mask on our own face before helping others, no one looks at him or her and thinks, "What a moron, I'm not going to do that. I'll just hold my breath and hope I don't pass out while I help other people." We shake our heads and go, "Okay, good advice, makes sense." If we are not okay, we will not be okay for anyone else.

SELF-FOCUS

"Keep your side of the sidewalk clean."

So if self-care is making sure that our own needs and wants are met, what does it mean when we are told to focus on ourselves? Where self-care is taking care of our insides, our bodies, our minds and hearts, when we practice self-focus, we focus on how we are behaving in the outside world. We begin to take responsibility for our own attitudes and behaviors and begin to change them so that we can respond to the world in a way that results in us feeling more empowered and at peace, and more comfortable in the world.

Focusing on oneself can be confusing and seem selfish and unrealistic to parents who are in the throes of crisis. I assure you that it is not selfish, and these things are the very things that can bring you out of a state of crisis. We're not talking about focusing on your needs and wants; that's self-care. We are talking about focusing on how you are behaving. Are you being the kind of person you want to be? The kind of parent, friend, partner? Instead of focusing on our child's behavior or anyone else's behavior, we begin to focus on our own behaviors. We start to look at how our own responses to things the world presents us with determine our own joy or misery. We start to see and feel the power; we get to decide how we will respond instead of just reacting without considering all our options and what might be best for ourselves. We begin to take responsibility for how we are choosing to experience the world.

We can learn how to be happy and sad at the same time and we can begin to find joy in our lives. Happiness and sadness are emotional responses to the world; peace and joy are emotional states of being protected from outside influences. When we choose to cultivate joy in our souls, we are better able to respond to the world around us, to find the balance between sadness and happiness. Bad things will always happen. It's a fact of life. Events will

HOW TO SURVIVE YOUR CHILD'S ADDICTION

make us happy, and events will make us sad. Sometimes one may be more present than the other. When we are joyful, we can keep our emotions in proper perspective and understand that emotions are temporary and that we have choices in every situation. We can be in charge even when we are not in control, and we can choose to move in a positive direction no matter where our compass lands.

The more we care for our own needs and feed our own physical and emotional energy supply, the better we will be able to address the needs of others. The more we cultivate joy and see how we are contributing to our own happiness and unhappiness, the more clarity we will get on what we have to change about ourselves, which, let's face it, is the only thing we have control over. When we begin to attend to our inner well-being and the role we play in the outer world, the hole in our soul begins to heal.

THE GIFTS OF PRACTICING
SOUL CARE

"The fuller we are, the more we have to give."

When I facilitate my parent support groups, I used to ask a fun, silly icebreaker question to get people to say something a bit more personal than their name and where they're from. One evening I asked, "What did you do for self-care this week?" It was amazing how challenging this question turned out to be. I think it was easier to answer what their most humiliating work experience was than to identify what they did to take care of themselves. It was such a challenge that I dropped the other sillier questions and continued to ask that at every meeting. One mother consistently listed all the things she did for her husband and her kids. Finally, one night after she completed her exhausting list of things she'd done that they should have been doing for themselves, I asked again, "What did you do for self-care for you?" She couldn't answer. She said taking care of others is her self-care. How many of you can relate?

Many parents fall into the trap of losing a sense of self-care as they are raising families. What I have seen is that addiction can perpetuate that well into adulthood, resulting in parents never reaching that point where their child needs less and less from them so that the parents can start to acknowledge their own needs and desires. Addiction can prevent the midlife crisis. As our kids become more independent, we suddenly start to look at our own lives and realize we've kind of lost them. Midlife crises get a bad rap because we associate them with a guy leaving his wife for a younger woman, but the truth is, it can be healthy to examine our lives and course-correct if we need to. That's exactly what recovery is all about, course correction, and one of the first corrections we usually find we have to make is to start really taking care of ourselves.

I'm not just talking about eating right and exercising, although those are ways to care for ourselves. I am talking about taking care of our emotional needs as well. We need to create a life that is fulfilling and peaceful. We need to learn how to find joy even when we're having a crappy day, or our child isn't doing well. I was talking to a mother of ten once and she said, "You're only as happy as your saddest child." It was the first time I had heard that expression and it stuck with me for a long time, and although I wasn't comfortable with it, I believed it. I know better now. We can be happier than our saddest child. We were born to be happier than our saddest child. It is not our responsibility as a parent to assume all the emotions of our children, our spouses, or our friends. It is our responsibility to tend to our own emotions, and when we do, we will have the energy to be supportive of those we love without losing ourselves.

I find that parents who have dealt with addiction, particularly those who grew up in a household with someone drinking or using, tend to feel like they have to be perfect and therefore in control, and that need for control can turn into an exaggerated sense of responsibility. Our sense of responsibility as a parent gets further distorted. We develop a tendency to try to fix everything for everybody. We begin to feel that if we don't do it, it won't get done or it won't get done correctly, which usually translates into it won't get done the way we want it (back to the control issue).

Our need to control makes us take on things that have nothing to do with us and are not our responsibility. I've coached many parents whose children ask them for money for stuff they should be paying for themselves, but I speak to just as many parents who offer to pay their adult kids' bills before the kid even asks because they just can't stay out of their kid's business.

Preventing your kid from feeling the consequences of their addiction does not decrease stress for the addict or take away their loneliness; it doesn't help them at all. All it does is it perpetuates their unhealthy behavior and causes stress for the parent. Of course, when we are so consumed with taking care of everything and everyone around us, we have no time to take care of ourselves and we forget that it's even an option or an actual responsibility of our own. Conveniently, it also becomes an excuse to not look at ourselves and how we are showing up in our lives.

- Are we spending more time thinking about someone else's behavior than we are thinking about our own behavior?

- Are we being patient and kind? Are we giving with love or are we playing a martyr?

- Are we micromanaging the people in our lives and their relationships?

- Are we acting like we know what's best for everyone when we clearly don't know what's best for ourselves?

It's much easier to look at how other people are behaving than to look at how we ourselves are behaving. We clutter our minds with things that don't belong to us and leave little room to take care of things that do belong to us and that often leads to a sense of powerlessness, which leads to a sense of chaos, and suddenly everything is a crisis, and our lives start to spiral out of control. Our efforts to control actually end up leaving us feeling completely out of control. Just think of how much energy you've put into trying to control your child and their disease. How in control do you feel of your life right now?

THE DOWNWARD SPIRAL TO DESPAIR

The **need to be perfect** leads to a **need to be in control** which leads to **an exaggerated sense of responsibility** which leads to a **feeling of martyrdom** which leads us to **feeling like we have no control** which leads us to **feel totally disempowered** which leads to **fear** that leads to **panic** which puts us in **crisis mode** and causes **frustration and resentment** because we can't control or fix what we are trying to.

So, how do we stop the spiral? Radical acceptance helps us start to see what we can and can't control where our child and their disease is concerned. The next step in radical acceptance is accepting all the other stuff in life that is not under our control. Once we accept this, the key is to then become hyper-focused on what we can control, namely our own behavior, and to build habits that result in us focusing on ourselves and creating a life that is so lovely that we no longer want to stick our nose into other people's lives. Where we once craved speaking to our addict every day, we can create a life where we crave the peace we get from not speaking to the addict every day. A life where we have so much peace and joy that we don't welcome the interruption from someone else's drama. There will always be times when we will have to be there for other people in difficult times, but we will stop seeking them out. Instead of surviving in chaos we begin thriving in peace, and chaos becomes undesirable. Where it was once our default, we realize that although we may have been hooked on drama at one point, we have no patience for it at this new point. This is where self-care and self-focus come in. We spend time focusing on building our own beautiful lives. How do we do this? We start with one new habit at a time.

GATEWAY DECISIONS

"We are our habits."

We've often heard that pot is a gateway drug. Alone it wasn't such a big deal, but once you were willing to smoke pot, it made you that much closer to being willing to try harder stuff. Many stoners would deny this, but research has proven it. It may not cause you to become addicted to other harder drugs but ask any pot smoker what else they've tried and chances are they would have a list.

Every day we make gateway decisions. They are those little decisions we make, often without thinking, that lead to sequential decisions that end up developing into habits. Think about it—you buy a box of donuts. You have one in the morning with coffee. You have one the next day. By the end of the box of donuts, having one with your coffee seems to be a thing, and it seems okay. Before you know it, you're consuming eight hundred calories of fat and sugar before you even get dressed, and this habit developed without you even noticing it. No real conscious decision was made. You're in the store, the donuts are on sale, and you pick up a pack. How do you think smokers got started? No one tries a cigarette thinking, "I can't wait to get addicted and get lung cancer." They figure, "Eh, I'll try it." They're not thinking about long-term ramifications.

It's important to look at the little gateway decisions we're making in our life, every day and to ask ourselves, "Is this a

119

gateway to misery or a gateway to joy? Does this gateway have a revolving door that will keep leading me back to where I am, or does it open onto a new, brighter path?" Take your mornings, for instance. How quickly do you reach for your phone in the morning? What is the first thing you check on your phone? Do you check to see if your child messaged you? Do you message them to make sure they're alive? If this resonates with you, then realize that reaching for your phone is a gateway decision. And, you guessed it—it has a revolving door in it. Checking your phone first thing in the morning allows your child's disease to command your day. Depending on whether you hear from them, you will either be relieved or terrified, but never actually joyful. Relief and joy are not the same things. They're not even close. A small decision like picking up the phone the moment we wake up determines the course of our whole day.

Other gateway decisions lead to behaviors that actually end up defining who we are. The Australian actor and teacher F. Matthias Alexander said, "People don't decide their futures; they decide their habits, and their habits decide their futures." Gateway decisions are what build our habits and our habits are what determine the quality of our lives. For us as parents, to really get our lives back, we need to get rid of old habits that result in chaos and misery and develop new habits that lead to a more peaceful and joyful life where we have enough emotional energy to not stop enjoying our lives when we face adversity. In Al-Anon they call it taking "life on life's terms." Giving up trying to control what we can't, everything except how we respond, and taking ownership over controlling what we can, how we respond. It sounds simple. Conceptually it is, but simple doesn't mean easy and habit building isn't easy. It takes consistency and persistence. Forget practice makes perfect. There is no perfect. Practice means progress, and progress is what we strive for. We are embarking on a journey to continually make our lives beautiful for as long as we have our lives. The goal is not just to fix what's broken. The goal is to make it better and stronger and to build a new way of thinking and behaving where our default is joy and peace, and the challenging moments are just that—moments. Some may be defining moments, but they will not define us. We get to define ourselves by how we respond to those moments.

We need to start paying very close attention to each decision we make. We start by looking at how we normally behave. We look at the decisions that we make on a daily basis. Then we start to categorize them—do they lead to joy or misery? Am I entering a pleasant path or a revolving door? It seems like a monumental task, but fear not. This is an area where baby steps have compounding effects and small changes can quickly lead to huge shifts. Some of these decisions will be around obvious behaviors, like picking up your phone before you're out of bed, while others will be less obvious. We'll start identifying how many of our thinking patterns are by choice as well. We'll learn that although we can't control our first thought, we can control our second thought. The little gateway decision to continue a negative thought pattern ends up leading us down the rabbit hole very quickly. Let's say you're used to waking up with an overwhelming feeling of dread. Without even specific thoughts of what might happen that day, you feel the dread. That's a conditioned response, and we'll work on that too. You feel the dread and then you have your first negative thought. "Joey's not going to make it to work today . . . and he's going to lose his job . . . and the stress of that is going to make him drink more . . . and he's never going to get sober . . . and I'm going to find him dead somewhere someday." I think we all know how quickly we can go from zero to one hundred when we are in crisis mode.

The problem is, we can end up in a perpetual state of crisis whether there is an actual crisis or not. This is where awareness of little gateway decisions comes in handy. You wake up with dread and you get right out of bed before that first thought has a chance to appear. The author and speaker Mel Robbins uses this in her Five Second Rule. She suggests counting, "Five, four, three, two, one," and then jumping out of bed. You're not going to want to, but you get to do it anyway. Once you're out of bed the thought process has been interrupted, and you can then make new little gateway decisions that bring you farther and farther away from the rabbit hole and toward the beautiful field filled with wildflowers where the rabbits hop around.

Now that we have a better understanding of the kinds of changes we need to make through Soul Care and how we have power over those changes through our gateway behaviors, we can start to look at how to actually go about making the changes. First, we have to work on the mindset needed to support these changes.

FAITH AND SPIRITUALITY -
ALLOWING OUR LIVES
TO HAVE PURPOSE
AND MEANING

*"We are all here for a reason, and we are
each a gift in and of ourselves."*

When I introduced Soul Care, I presented two elements. Self-care was the internal or personal element and self-focus was the external element—how we relate to ourselves and how we relate to the world. We are each an individual being and an integral part of a larger world. How we live our lives has an effect on everything around us. We can be an instrument of joy or misery, for ourselves and for others. We have a responsibility to ourselves *and* to our world as well.

In order to start caring for our souls, we have to examine our basic belief system because this will determine how we relate to ourselves and the outside world. When I say belief system, I'm not referring to a belief system regarding God. Albert Einstein said, "I think the most important question facing humanity is, 'Is the universe a friendly place?'" This isn't likely a question we often or ever actually ask ourselves, but we have developed an answer consciously or not. Our answer to this question determines our whole outlook on life. Einstein goes on to assert that if we feel the universe is unfriendly then we will operate from a place of fear and insecurity, and we will behave in a defensive and self-serving manner, trying not to participate in the world. If we feel that the universe is neutral then we become victims of circumstance, and our lives lack meaning. But, if we believe the universe is actually friendly, then our sense of safety and security will come from being an active part of the universe. Do you feel like a participant in the world or a victim of it?

In order to bring ourselves out of the crisis and chaos of addiction and to believe that we do in fact have power in our lives, it is vital that we see ourselves as part of the world around us and assess how we relate to this world. Our world can be defined as small as our immediate family or as broad as the people of the earth. I find it better to start close to home. The better we begin to relate to our close-knit world, the easier it will become to relate to the world on a broader scale and the more valuable a part of the larger world we will begin to feel.

Faith usually has a positive connotation. We often interchange it with hope and say things like, "Have faith," meaning, trust things will work out the way you want. If our view of the world is generally negative, however, we end up with the faith that things will not go as we want and that we are doomed to misery. I think of faith as our internal belief system, be it positive or negative, while spirituality is how that system manifests in our behaviors. How we practice what we believe. It's how we allow our internal beliefs to influence how we behave. Whether we consider ourselves spiritual or not, we all have a belief system and if it is negative, those negative beliefs will come out in our behaviors. As we begin to care for our souls, we must make sure that our innermost beliefs are aligned with our desire for joy and peace.

In Part 1 of this book, when we talked about radical acceptance that our child is an addict, and that we cannot control their
disease, there was no need for faith or spiritual belief. It was as
factual as the sky being above us, the ground being below us, and
water being in the oceans. In my experience, being able to find
peace and joy in our own lives after accepting these facts takes a
lot of faith. For many parents, the starting point is so grim that
it's hard to imagine ever finding joy again or ever experiencing
peace. This is where I say we may have to fake it until we make
it again. We have to allow for the possibility and proceed as if
it's possible, even if we're not convinced it is. We can't hold off
making changes until we believe. As we make the changes and
feel the results, we come to believe without realizing it.

It is often said in the recovery world that addiction is a disease
of the body, mind, and spirit. I would say most of our woes in this
world are in fact issues where body, mind, and spirit are discon-
nected. This is the hole in the soul that requires Soul Care. If we
can get our body, mind, and spirit aligned, we have the confidence
to move out of our comfort zones, make tough decisions, and
create a life we actually love, one that is fulfilling and joyful, even
if those we love are still struggling. This goes for everyone, whether
they are dealing with addiction or not. It is the basis of major
religions and spiritual teachings as well as eastern and western
philosophies. We have a choice: if we don't love our lives, we can
stay stuck or we can change our lives. There are always choices.
Finding joy is a choice. Even if it is served up on a silver platter,
if we choose not to see it then we won't. I'll rephrase that—if
we choose to look only at the negative in life, we will miss all the
positive things that life is also presenting us with. When we have
been worn away by a child's addiction, this can be hard to see and
understand. The universe feels very unfriendly and very uncaring;
we become defensive and victimized and isolate ourselves from
life. We stop taking care of ourselves, doing things we enjoy, and

we shirk our responsibilities to ourselves. We develop a negative belief system, whether we are aware of it or not, and that belief system causes us to behave in ways that cause our lives to become self-fulfilling prophecies of negativity.

My years in the rooms of twelve-step meetings and parent groups and my work with private clients have shown me how common it is for people to have a resistance to the idea of faith. Negative experiences with religion growing up seem to be the biggest culprit, whether from the home or the institution. As children, we are vulnerable and susceptible to fear so if we are taught that fear is part of faith and spirituality, it makes sense that we reject it. Faith is often associated with the dogma of a given religion or denomination built around a punitive god or a god to whom one should feel completely accountable. Feelings of guilt, shame, and martyrdom can stem from these misconceptions and the associated behaviors greatly limit our ability to align our body, mind, and spirit, resulting in a constant inner struggle and the resistance to the very things that can bring us joy and peace.

I am someone whose default is joy. I want to be happy and I want to spread joy. Years ago, I would have said, "And I want to make people happy." Recovery has taught me that I cannot make anyone happy except me. I can be joyful and spread positive energy, what people do with that is none of my business and out of my control. I am Catholic. I was raised Catholic and had a very positive experience with the church. Not all good but good enough. My mother was raised in a convent after her own mother became ill when she was five. Given the time, the late 1920s in Brooklyn, I have to assume she had a bunch of strict, conservative Irish Catholic nuns right off the boat, as they say. By the time I hit Catholic school in the early '70s, the nuns weren't even in habits. My mother once said, and I will quote her, "I don't understand. All they do is teach you to love this and love that. You're not learning any catechism at all." It always makes me chuckle that she was dismayed that I was being taught love. My mother was a very loving person, but she was taught that her knowledge of the dogma of religion was more important than her relationship with God. Her God was more punitive than loving and the love between her and God was not a touchy-feely personal love like what I was being taught.

When my husband was killed, the priest asked me to pick the readings for his funeral. I remember asking him to please pick them himself. I told him that at that point, my comfort came from my faith in humanity, not from scripture. As much as I am comfortable with the concept of God with a capital G, my real faith comes from my experiences in the world, my experiences with other people. My joyful default has allowed me to see the world in a very positive light.

Mr. Rogers told the story that when there was an accident or a tragedy, his mother would tell him to look for the helpers. I cried the first time I heard this as an adult because I felt like somebody finally understood me. I have always seen the good. When my husband was killed, my children and I experienced humanity at its best, and that's what we focused on. I watched as others focused on the tragedy and loss instead of how the world had rallied to help, and it perpetuated their suffering, keeping them in a state of fear, sadness, anger, and negativity, preventing them from moving on and embracing the life that they still had. I also remember being driven home the evening of his death, and as we crossed the 59th Street bridge heading from Manhattan to Queens, I looked south toward the smoke billowing from where the Towers had stood earlier that morning and thought, "Wow, it was Anthony's time to go. But it wasn't mine. I guess I have to figure out how to live without him." I was devastated, but I didn't want this to be the end of my joy or my children's joy, and as tragic and traumatic as the loss of my husband and their father was, and through all the shock and pain and confusion, I knew we would be joyful again. I wanted us to be joyful again. I made a decision at that moment, to choose joy. I vowed to give my children as good a life as I would be able to. I share this with you because the idea of faith is a very personal thing and need not be shied away from. It's basically an acceptance that things will be what they will be and a trust that there will always be an opportunity for us to be okay. Life may not go the way we want, but we can find opportunity and joy if we choose to.

In twelve-step programs like Al-Anon, we sometimes say, if nothing else, we can have faith in the power of the group, and at times, the group can hold space for our faith until we find it. That's the faking it part; we may not believe it yet, but we allow for the possibility that we can be okay and then behave as if we believe. I didn't know how I was going to help my family through the death of my husband, their father, but I was determined to. I didn't see a way out for my son or for me, but I had faith that my own life was meant for more than the despair I felt. I had faith that there was enough good in the world that somehow, I would find peace and joy again. I took the advice I was given and I turned my son over to those who had the best chance of helping him, and then I did whatever I needed to do to help myself. I had no idea what my future would hold, but I had faith that it would hold something better.

If faith is an innermost belief, spirituality is how we relate that to the outside world. For me, a sense of spirituality is a simple awareness that it's not all about me. I am but a small part of something much bigger, all interrelated and interdependent. And even if I am a small part, I can still have a profound impact on a small or big scale. Sometimes my spirituality practice can be a discussion with God about a decision I have to make, sometimes I just appeal to the universe for help or guidance, and sometimes I stand on my lawn and summon a cardinal to show me its colors and I feel incredibly connected to the world around me and grateful to be a part of it. My spirituality is the practice of my faith. My faith is the belief that I can be happy if I choose to be. Through my spirituality, I put this belief into practice by embracing my humble place in the world and collaborating with the universe to help me focus on what I can do to make my best contribution, and in doing so, I find my peace and my joy.

Relinquishing responsibility for our addicted child's disease in order to give them the space to take their own responsibility for it, admitting that we cannot fix it for them, and being aware that they may not be able to fix it themselves can be incredibly difficult. It's a decision that can cause so many mixed emotions. Guilt, fear, frustration, and overwhelming sadness can consume us. I will venture to say that it would be completely unbearable to do this without a sense of faith and spiritual connection. Just as the addict lacks a spiritual connection, we as parents can lose sight of our own spirituality. To be able to do the tough work it will take to get our lives back, we have to find it. We need to have our own positive connection with the world. When we are able to feel this connection we can move forward in faith, knowing that we will always have the ability to choose joy.

In the next section we will explore some practices that, with the help of gateway decisions, allow us to begin to shift our inner belief systems to view the world as a friendlier place that we want to be a part of. Notice we develop the practices in order to shift our beliefs, not the other way around. These practices are what shift our beliefs, and when we are able to shift our beliefs, we change our own perception of reality. This is what people mean when they say you can change your reality. We always create our reality whether we are aware of it or not. We do this through our perception and through our responses. We may not be able to change our circumstances, but how we perceive the world and how we respond to it determine our reality. If you respond like a powerless victim, then your reality will be that of a victim.

If you respond as an empowered person and make choices to better your circumstances, then your reality will be that of an empowered person.

This may sound a bit "out there" but here is a simple example of how we create our own realities all the time. My children think Will Ferrell is hilarious. I don't find him hilarious. The reality of my kids' world is that Will Ferrell is hilarious. The reality of my world is that he isn't. Will Ferrell is Will Ferrell no matter what; how we each perceive him is what determines how he exists in each of our worlds; in other words, how we perceive him determines our reality. To some people, vanilla is the best flavor, to other people vanilla is the most boring flavor. The same flavor plays a different role in different realities when it's perceived differently. By bringing the following practices into our daily lives, we are proving to ourselves that we can feel differently even if nothing changes but our own perceptions and responses. We alter our reality. When we do this with intention, we get to define our reality and make it something that brings us joy and peace where not only are we better, but we can serve the world better as well.

OUR SOMATIC STATE

"Before there are words, there is the wordless communication of the body." —*Michael Changaris, Psy.D.*

It's worth noting at this juncture that our bodies can work against us as we try to reset our behaviors and our thinking, and we have to be mindful of our somatic or physical state. Our somatic state is determined by how our body responds to the world around us. We've talked about how our minds react, but that feeling in the pit of our stomach when the phone rings, that's a somatic response. The clenched jaw and frozen shoulders are all somatic responses. Think of a cat's hair straight up on end. When our bodies are in a state of contraction or stress, it's impossible to destress the mind.

Look at what athletes do before the start of their event, whether it's a race or a game. They often shake their bodies, roll their necks, or straighten their shoulders. Speechmakers do similar things. Deep breaths, powerful exhales. Each of these things is a way of the body telling the brain that it's safe and okay to do whatever it is that they are about to do. It is a way of intentionally controlling their somatic state so that their brains receive the message they want them to receive. If a high diver is getting ready to jump, his mind is going to go "What, are you crazy? That's not safe!" Those thoughts cause the diver to contract his body to protect it and can cause him to hold his breath as a reaction to fear. By controlling his breath and relaxing his body, he's telling his brain that it's okay and that he is actually safe, even if his mind was fearful.

Amy Cuddy is well known for her talks on power poses and faking it until you make it, where she talks about putting yourself in a powerful pose to alter your somatic state. Research studies have shown that our hormone levels change with these poses. Try this exercise. Hunch your shoulders in front of you as if you're bracing against the wind and clench your jaw tightly. Now tell yourself that you are a strong and powerful person who feels joy and is in charge of your life. It's kind of hard to feel it and believe it when your body is in a defensive and protective state. Now stand up tall, puff out your chest, smile, and say the same words. It feels far more possible. We have to be acutely aware of our somatic state as we work on learning new skills and make sure that our bodies are in a state to allow us to receive and feel the benefits of the practices.

I'll offer some simple practices to adjust your somatic state as you practice these tools. First, become aware of your body. Even as I'm sitting and writing this book, I find I may check in with myself multiple times an hour to make sure my jaw is relaxed and my shoulders are down. It's easy to get excited and lean in, but that can send the wrong signal to my brain and tell my brain that there is danger or stress present, and my creativity and thoughts won't flow under stress. I have to consciously relax, constantly.

We talked earlier about paying attention to our gut reactions. This is where we get to see if our gut reactions are coming from a place of fear, a place of legitimacy, or if it's coming from a place where you're telling yourself a story that just isn't true. We get to assess if there is real danger causing the fear and even if there is, if it is worth the risk, as in the high dive. In that case we can override the gut reaction by controlling the state of our body. If your kid asks you to buy them groceries and you get that feeling of dread in your stomach, you can notice it and ask yourself, "What will happen if I say no? Will something bad actually happen, or am I just afraid something bad will happen?" When you realize that you have no proof that something bad will happen, you can take a deep breath, relax your shoulders, and tell your mind that it's okay to say no and send your brain the signal that it's okay. Being able to get our minds and bodies aligned is a very powerful tool that can help us make healthy decisions.

Right now, take inventory. Which parts of your body are clenched? Where are your muscles contracted? Now, close your eyes and take a couple of deep breaths. Breathe into those areas and on the exhale, relax those muscles. Sometimes it helps to tighten them even more and then relax them. Practice this. Get into the habit of checking in with yourself throughout the day. When you feel good, check in and see if you are tensed up anywhere. When you're feeling stressed, check in. I find when I relax my jaw, I press my tongue against the roof of my mouth instead, so I am aware to make sure I don't replace one contraction with another. My apartment tends to be cold so I check in, and if I'm tensed up I assess whether I'm stressed or cold. If I find I'm cold, then I bundle up. Regardless of the reason for our contracted somatic state, the negative effect is the same. We have to continuously work on getting our bodies into a more relaxed state as often as possible.

A sensory box is a great tool to use when trying to adjust your somatic state. To create a sensory box, collect things that are pleasant to all your senses. I suggest something in your favorite color or something that you love to look at. It can be a postcard or a picture of a flower, anything that you think is beautiful. Then find something that feels nice to touch, a piece of soft fabric or a smooth stone. I keep a piece of velvet in my favorite color that excites two senses for me. Then have something that smells wonderful to you. It can be a piece of paper with perfume, cologne, essential oil, or a candle. When I was a child, too young to wear lip gloss, I used to keep a strawberry-flavored lip gloss in my desk at school and when I felt nervous or sleepy, I would pull it out and smell it and feel uplifted. Next, find something you can taste. It can be a little piece of chocolate or hard candy, sweet or sour. Depending on your taste, it can be a salt or sugar packet. The point is to have something on hand that delights your sense of taste. Also, have on hand an auditory resource. It can be a favorite song saved to your phone or an app with pleasant sounds. You might like the sound of rain or of waves. I love Tibetan bowl and gong sounds and have an app that plays them. Lastly, have a photograph that represents sheer bliss to you. A photo that makes you feel the way you always want to feel. Not one that is too nostalgic that it ends up bittersweet. Find a photo that simply sparks joy. Now, put all of these things you've collected in a box or a basket and consider this sensory box your recovery emergency kit. If you are trying to relax your physical state and are having trouble, use these things to delight your senses and help you relax your somatic state so you can reap the maximum benefits of the following practices.

SPIRITUAL PRACTICES

"If there was a perfect prayer it would be thank you."

Developing a routine of spiritually minded practices is critical to our ability to step out of chaos and find peace, even if you're still in the fake-it phase. Morning routines help us begin to reclaim our days, one day at a time, by not allowing addiction to set the tone for our day, as it has for so long. Evening routines allow us to go to sleep in peace so that our sleep can be restorative and not fraught with disruption and worry. We are adding spiritual tools to our toolbox. The more tools or practices we have to choose from, the more equipped we will be to respond to any situation in a healthy manner. If one doesn't work, we try another. The more tools we have, the more likely we are to find one that works. The more practice we get using these tools, the more we hone our skills. When we become aware of our gateway decisions, we can use these tools to avoid the revolving door. Habit stacking, practicing as many of these things as possible daily, as part of our morning and evening routines can change us in ways we might not be able to imagine. Soon our gateway decisions will default to healthier ones and these practices will help us get to a better place where we step out of crisis mode and find peace. They help us define and align our inner system of beliefs to be more positive, and from this positive place, we can make better decisions in our lives, and when we are better, everyone around us benefits.

GRATITUDE AND APPRECIATION

A gratitude practice is the basic building block of positive spirituality. No matter how much things suck, we can always find something to be grateful for. This may seem obvious to some of you, but how often do you actually do it? How often do you use gratitude to get yourself out of a funk or to get you through something really hard? Showing gratitude may not change our circumstances, but it can have a huge effect on how we perceive our circumstances. We will still have trials to deal with but having an attitude of gratitude can help us manage our trials with more strength and peace. As we begin to acknowledge all the good things we do have in our lives, it starts to put our struggles into perspective. Here are several gratitude practices we can incorporate into our routines.

A gratitude journal is a great first step for a lot of people. Actually writing down three things you're grateful for in the morning and in the evening is a great routine. In the beginning, you may only be able to think of the big obvious things. I'm grateful I have a home, a job, food, and a family. I usually ask clients to write down three things that they can see or touch, right where they are; in other words, mundane things to be grateful for. It can be as simple as the fact that they have shoes and a roof over their heads. Sometimes it's the glass of water next to them. Eventually they can start looking out the window and see a blue sky, or a bird, or a pretty cloud. You can also find gratitude journals that have writing prompts to help you focus on things you're grateful for that you may take for granted or not notice.

Adding the words *thank you* to your gratitude practice can bring it to a whole new level. Being grateful makes us appreciate what we have. Showing appreciation by saying *thank you* makes us feel connected to the provider of those things. When we acknowledge that there is a force greater than ourselves that has allowed all these things to exist in our lives, including the opportunities for us to gather these things, we are connecting with that greater force. This is the crux of spirituality and one of the simplest ways to ease into a spiritual practice. By speaking the words *thank you*, we allow ourselves to develop a tangible sense of connection. It helps us feel like we are collaborating with the world around us instead of being victimized by it. *Thank you* is one of the most powerful phrases we can utter.

As we start doing our gratitude list on a regular basis, we begin to realize there are tons of small things that we're grateful for: a sunny day, a dog, a good bagel, no traffic, a friend we run into. Slowly, as we start to list more than three things, we start to see our lives a little differently. It may start to feel a little less bleak. When we are dealing with a child suffering from addiction, our thinking often gets as distorted as theirs and our worlds become very small. We isolate and obsess. We prioritize our child's disease over everything else in our lives. Our other relationships suffer, leaving us feeling alone even when we are surrounded by friends and family, and we think of little else than our child's behavior and disease. We become so emotionally overwhelmed that the most mundane tasks can be completely overwhelming. We become despondent and we stop looking for the good. Without anything to feel good about, we lose all concept of joy. I ask parents what brings them joy and most of the time, they can't come up with an answer. Joy has become elusive and seemingly impossible. I get it, but it's not! It is truly possible if you choose to want it. A gratitude journal is a perfect way to start seeing the good in our lives, even when there is still some bad stuff.

Feeling grateful in the morning and at bedtime is fundamental to shifting our thinking to change our belief system. We begin to feel that things actually can get better by proving to ourselves that things aren't completely horrible. Gratitude practices help us see that despite whatever tough stuff is going on, there is also good stuff going on. It helps us regain a sense of balance in our lives between the good that exists and the challenges that exist. As you get more practice, you will start to develop an attitude of gratitude where gratitude gets coded into your DNA, and you won't have to remind yourself to practice anymore.

I was at a soul-sucking job a few years ago. My subway ride to work was like a march to the gallows. I hated feeling that way, so until I could leave the job, which I did the next year, I worked hard on my attitude. If I was on the train and I started stressing, I'd look for my favorite color, chartreuse. It's a bright green, a very happy color. I'd look for someone whose makeup looked nice. I would start noticing shoes and clothes that I liked. As I would notice these things, I would say a little thank you to the universe for letting me see the beauty around me, and I would say a little blessing for all the people on the train with me. My mood was altered immediately. Gratitude is more than a practice; it's a tool that you can and should use whenever you feel the negativity monsters creeping in.

Years ago, I was getting ready to do a very unpleasant task for one of the alcoholics in my life. She had taken a fall, was admitted to the hospital via ambulance, and left a mess behind in her apartment. I made the decision to take care of it, partly to spare her children from dealing with it and mostly because I thought it was the compassionate thing to do, given the circumstances. In my mind, the fall had to do with her drinking, so there were a lot of negative emotions swirling around in my head and I was dreading it. I decided that I had to approach it with compassion and the best way for me to do that was to start with gratitude. I literally stood in my apartment and wrote down a bunch of things I was grateful for, including being grateful for the fact that I was able to do this for her, that I'm not an alcoholic and that after it's done, I still have my lovely life to return to. I put the piece of paper into my pocket, decided to take the ferry uptown, and made it a point to enjoy the boat ride. By the time I got to her apartment, my mood was great, and I had no problem approaching the task at hand with compassion for the person I love who has a dreadful disease. The task was still very unpleasant but the way I experienced it was completely different. In the end I was grateful for the opportunity to do something kind. Practice until gratefulness becomes your default.

HEALTHY COMPASSION

Like gratitude, empathy and compassion are building blocks of spirituality. They allow us to step out of ourselves and our own suffering and look at a situation from another person's perspective. Empathy is an attempt to see a situation through another person's eyes and to try to understand where they are coming from. Compassion is empathy coupled with a desire to help. This is where the waters can get murky. When I teach compassion, I emphasize that we can have compassion without taking responsibility. We may find ourselves wanting to help, but we have to ask ourselves if we *should* help. Someone wanting help and someone needing help are two different things. If we have a tendency to jump in and help, whether we are asked to or not, or if we are asked and don't want to, then our motive is not compassion but something else. It could end up enabling or intrusive. It could end up causing us to be resentful. I teach healthy compassion where we check our desire to help and consider what helping may actually look like. This comes up a lot with my clients, and it's usually around their kids taking responsibility for stuff. Say your son never brings his keys and is always locked out. He calls you and expects you to drop what you're doing to bring him the keys.

You can be compassionate for his plight of being locked out and not take on the responsibility of bringing him keys. You can have compassion for your daughter because she doesn't have money for her phone bill because she's spending it all on drugs and still not pay her bill.

With regard to our addicted child, healthy compassion allows us to separate our child from his disease. We can have compassion for the afflicted while not supporting the addiction when we can accept that they are suffering and at war with themselves. Healthy compassion allows for connection without anger or resentment. When I was able to step back and accept that my son was suffering so much pain and anguish, I was able to stop being mad at him and just feel compassion for him. I was also able to start feeling compassion for myself and my other children for all that we had suffered as a result. I was not the only one feeling the pain. We all were, and when we could acknowledge the pain together, we were able to start the healing as a family. I was able to help, just in different ways than I realized. If I had stayed in my own pain without developing healthy compassion for everyone else, we couldn't have healed.

In order for us to begin to practice healthy compassion, we have to understand that everything isn't about us. It is almost impossible for us to feel compassion when we are on the defensive and feel wronged. We have to stop taking everything personally and acting like everything is a personal assault. Most people are not thinking about us. We may be the center of our own universe, but we are not the center of other people's universes. Other people's behavior is not about us. Our child's disease is not about us. Most of what happens to us is not personal. It just happens as it happens, and we happen to be there. The rude person in line would have been rude to anyone standing there. The train wasn't late to screw you over. It was just late. We have to recognize when we are in martyr mode or victim mode and step out of it. Think of the person that asks, "Why does this always happen to me?" The chances are the thing just happened. Even when it is a loved one directing horrible, hurtful things directly at us, making it feel as personal as possible, it's still about them and what they're processing and how they're reacting to their own pain. Hurt people hurt people. Them trying to cause us pain is not about us. When we understand this, we can have compassion. Al-Anon has a great slogan: QTIP, quit taking it personally. It's not about you.

When we stop taking things personally and we stop making it all about us, we can start to look at the other person with compassion. Where are they coming from? What is their pain point? Am I showing up for them the way they need me to? By approaching another with compassion, we leave more room for understanding and loving and less room for resentment and anger. It allows us to actually show up for them. Often when we are dealing with our addict, we are furious, frustrated, and terrified, and we just want to fix it. Parents often tell me they want to shake their kid or smack some sense into them, or they just want them out. The truth is, we love our kids. As hard as it is to like them, we do love them. We have to always remember how much we love them. If we can put ourselves in a mindset of compassion, we can reconnect with the child abducted by the disease and show caring and understanding. That doesn't mean accepting unacceptable behavior. But as loving parents, when we act toward our kids without compassion, it doesn't feel right at some basic level. Whether we are aware of it or not, it causes dissonance because we want to love them but it's as if we don't know how to anymore. We can love our child and hate their disease. We can feel compassion for their suffering and hold them accountable for their behavior. Taking responsibility is about us. Compassion is about them. We can love them deeply and still have clear boundaries.

I was helping a client whose child was making unreasonable requests of her. Her son was asking her to serve all of his meals to him in his room. She wanted to know how to say no with compassion. This wasn't a question of compassion for her son, but it was a matter of compassion for herself. Her son was capable of going to the kitchen. He didn't want to go to the kitchen because he was using drugs and filled with anxiety and wouldn't go for the help his mother had offered him. If she continued to bring him his meals, why would he go for help? He was getting everything he wanted. He was using drugs and taking no responsibility and feeling no consequences. I suggested that if she did not think that continuing to serve him was in her best interest, then she could say no. A simple no is neither a compassionate nor an uncompassionate response. It's a neutral response to a request that made my client uncomfortable and one that she did not want to say yes to. Avoiding making someone unhappy and accepting unacceptable behavior is not the same as compassion. Compassion is an active emotion, not a passive one. Avoidance is passive. A no in this situation was simply a boundary, and boundaries involve self-compassion.

As we practice compassion, it is vital to remember to practice self-compassion. Parenting a child in addiction is really hard and really painful. We've all gone through our own version of hell, and we need kindness and compassion too. Self-compassion includes forgiving ourselves for the times we may realize we may not have done the best thing. Remember, we've all done the best we could do at the time we did it. We haven't had it easy. That's not playing the martyr or the victim card; it's a statement of fact. Dealing with a child in addiction is absolutely horrible and heartbreaking. We have tried everything we could think of to fix this or to save ourselves. We did our best. Our goal in recovery is to make our best better so that moving forward, our actions and decisions get better.

On a broader spiritual level, compassion allows for deep connections with the world around us. It helps us see our place in the world and understand that that place is not in the center of it. It's okay to be the center of our own world as long as we understand that we are not the center of everyone else's world. When we have compassion for others, we can let go of resentments and instead understand that most people are doing their best. We can understand that we all struggle, some of us more than others, and some of us with less ability to handle it than others. Compassion allows for kindness, and kindness is basic to humanity and spirituality. When was the last time we were actually kind to our addicted child? Often when I start working with clients, they find that it's been a long time since they treated their child with compassion. It's hard to see the wounded child underneath the horrible behavior. Compassion allows us to do this. Compassion allows us to feel more connected, and when we feel more connected, we are more inclined to want to be a more active participant in the world. We need to show up in life as the best version of ourselves so that we can have the best impact on the world and feel connected.

When building your sense of compassion, remember:

- QTIP: Quit taking it personally.
- Things usually don't happen to you. They just happen.
- People are generally doing their best.
- We never know what someone else is going through, just like people don't know what we are going through.
- Compassion allows us to empathize with others and drives us to do better.
- Compassion allows us to connect with people on a deeper level.

- Compassion helps alleviate resentment.

- Compassion helps us to be kind.

- We can be kind and compassionate and still maintain healthy boundaries.

- Compassion helps us connect with the world around us and is fundamental to our spirituality.

- We can start by being compassionate with ourselves. Having an addicted child is really hard. We all do our best, and if you're reading this book, then you're trying to make your best better.

SERVICE

Help is not a four-letter word. We talk a lot about not helping our child as if helping is a bad thing in and of itself. The rule of thumb is that we are not helping if we are doing for others what they can and should do for themselves. If compassion is empathy plus a desire to help, then the more compassion we can feel on a broader scale, the more we will be called to be of service on a broader scale. What we consider broad can be subjective. If we have been fully self-absorbed and are trying to get connected to people around us, we can start to volunteer for instance. If we do a twelve-step or other kind of support group, service is usually highly encouraged. Sometimes we can volunteer to greet people, lead a meeting, or prepare coffee for after the meeting. Sometimes we may be compelled by a tragedy or disaster to send money or volunteer to donate or collect supplies. It is part of human nature to want to connect and being of service has been shown to have both mental and physical benefits.

When we are of service, we feel more connected. We feel less isolated and develop a stronger sense of belonging. It can increase our feeling of self-worth and can increase our gratitude for things in our own life. It can empower us if we are of service to causes that we care about. It can make us feel useful in situations where we have little actual control. It gets us out of our own heads and can help us gain perspective regarding how we fit in the world. It can help increase a sense of meaning and purpose in our lives.

When we can be of service in a healthy way, the world becomes a more welcoming place, and we can begin to feel more at home in it. We begin to alter our belief systems and grow our spirituality. The great thing is, we get to decide how we want to be of service. We get to help on our own terms. We get to decide where and when we want to be of service. When we operate from a place of joy and confidence and within a system of healthy boundaries, being of service can be one of the most beneficial things we can do. It promotes all elements of Soul Care and feeds our spiritual growth.

The idea of being of service at a time when we may feel completely overwhelmed by life may seem unreasonable. Taking on some big volunteer project may not be feasible for several reasons, and that's fine. We can start small. We can start with little random acts of kindness. We can hold the door for people. We can put down our cell phones and smile at the clerk as they ring us up at the store. We can say hello and thank you to the bus driver. Anytime we spread positive energy and good feelings, we feel better too. Remember the Golden Rule: treat others the way you want to be treated. It can start immediately.

I have three big dogs and I scoop a lot of poop every day. If I'm picking up after my own dogs and I see a pile someone else should have picked up, I usually pick that up too. It's my little way of making my world a better place without taking on an exaggerated sense of responsibility.

When I used to drive my kids home from school in Manhattan, it would often be at the same time the taxis were going off duty.

Traffic getting onto the Queensborough bridge would be hectic and I would often let the cabbies go ahead of me. I would point out to my kids that while we were in no rush, these guys had to get to the garage in time to hand over the cab. They didn't know that I was intentionally trying to help them out and I don't know that it ever really made a difference, but it made me feel good. It made me feel like I was connecting to the world and in tune with different dynamics, and it showed my kids how easy it is to be nice.

What we foster grows and what we give comes back to us. Think about the last time you were angry and lost your cool with someone. Did you feel better or worse? Even if you felt vindicated, did you actually feel more positive after? Chances are that you didn't feel better. Now think of the last time you made someone smile just by being kind. How good did that make you feel? We can start being of service just by being nicer to everyone we deal with. A smile here or there can have a ripple effect for us and for the person who felt our good energy.

I also find that the nicer we are, the better people respond to us. People prefer upbeat, pleasant people to unpleasant people. The more people respond to us positively, the more we come to expect people to respond to us positively. It starts to become the norm. We start to alter our belief systems to believe that people are generally pleasant. We start to shift our reality as people become nicer. Then if we encounter an unpleasant person, we recognize that as the outlier. We don't take it personally and we can let it go more easily because we no longer internalize it. We learn to focus on the positive things that make us feel good instead of the negative things that make us feel bad. At some point, I have my clients come up with a plan of service that suits them. Although they often start with simple goals, such as one random act of kindness per day, the feelings they experience are so rewarding that they build on it and kindness becomes a vital part of all their behaviors. When we are kind, we are being of service to ourselves and all those around us.

MEDITATION

"When we pray, we ask. When we meditate, we hear the answers."

I'm sure we've all heard about the benefits of meditation and how helpful it is for our minds and bodies. When it's said that meditation helps relieve stress and anxiety, notice that it doesn't say that meditation fixes problems. It doesn't claim to relieve stress by eliminating stressors. As we've seen before, pain is inevitable; suffering is not. The existence of stressors and triggers is inevitable; suffering stress and anxiety is optional. Meditation can help.

There are other things that meditation can do as well. Meditation is a way of quieting the noise caused by addiction by allowing us to focus on something else, and that ten minutes without noise can be tremendously helpful in restoring some clarity and filling our often depleted well of emotional energy. Think about this and be honest with yourself. How often do you have a quiet ten minutes, not on your phone and not spent worrying, but an actual ten minutes of peace? Not ten minutes in bed avoiding getting up. Ten minutes at peace. For many of us it becomes elusive in a hectic world because we rely on the world to provide peace for us. When we practice self-focus, we realize that we are responsible for the feeling of peace in our lives, which means we have the power to create it.

I find it helpful to set up a little sacred space in my home for meditation. I often work with my clients on this. It can be a corner of a room or a little table in a hallway. One of my clients had a small wooden table that had belonged to her mother and had been handed down to her. She just couldn't bear to get rid of it. It was too small to be of much use and she only remembered it holding a little vase when her mother was alive. She pulled it out of her garage and decided to liven up the little table. She painted it her favorite color, a turquoise blue, and it became her sacred space. She found a spot in the corner of her bedroom and set it up. She put her favorite candle on it and added some stones with inspiring words inscribed on them. She put an essential oil diffuser and, in honor of her mother, a small vase for flowers. Above it, she hung a small shelf with the books she would use for her morning readings. Every morning, when she got out of bed, the first thing she would do was sit on the floor in front of her little table and meditate for a few minutes. It wasn't easy for her at first. We worked on a few different ways she could center and be present. For me, the most important part of meditation is just being present in the moment for a few moments. That ability to give yourself even three minutes without allowing all the stress and worry to bombard you can be incredibly powerful. It was for my client. Once she got into a routine, I could see that she was less tense every time I saw her. She was so shocked by the immediate effect that she started meditation in the evening too. She said that whenever she had to talk with her addicted daughter she would sit in front of her little table and meditate for three minutes first.

Although there is no right or wrong way to meditate, which means there are a million ways to do it, when we are used to operating in a state of chaos, the idea of calm can be intimidating and hard to process. It's easy to be cynical that when life is so incredibly difficult, ten minutes of peaceful contemplation can make a difference. I assure you it can. Some hard things in life are inevitable; living in a constant state of chaos is optional. Below, I've included some tips on meditating. You can try different ways of meditating or just practice being still. Once you find a method you like, actually do it. The benefits of meditation are cumulative; after all, you're retraining your thinking. You don't get into shape in the first week of going to the gym. It takes patience to meditate and patience to keep up the practice, like any other habit we try to develop. Start small and steady to grow big.

1. Breathe. We all breathe, but how often do we pay attention to our breath? Slowing our breath, extending our diaphragm, and releasing our shoulders actually has a positive effect on our parasympathetic nervous system. Slowing down our breathing tells the brain that we are safe so the brain responds by making us feel calmer by sending out calming hormones. Look at the power we have here. We are controlling the messages our body parts are sending each other just by controlling our breath. If the only thing you do is breathe deeply and slowly for three to five minutes each morning, that would be an amazing meditation.

2. You don't have to clear your mind to meditate. The point is to put your mind and body into a relaxed state. Why do you think we count sheep to fall asleep? It's a form of meditation. Saying the Rosary, chanting prayers, or using prayer beads are the same thing. Focusing on one thing or on repetition has the same effect. You can meditate by deep breathing and staring at a house plant for five minutes and just notice all the shades of green and brown. What does the dirt look like? Are there stones in it or fallen leaves? What color is the pot it's in? If your mind drifts, just bring it back. Don't get frustrated. It takes practice. This is a practice in being present in the moment.

3. You don't have to be still or have quiet to meditate. You can go for a walk, paying attention to your breath and focusing your thoughts on something positive. Or you can walk and focus on the sounds around you. They can be city sounds or nature sounds. It doesn't matter. Just breathe and focus. I hate standing in line for anything. If I absolutely have to do it, I will meditate this way while I do. I'll close my

eyes and just listen to all the sounds around me, or if I'm
in a grocery store, I may focus on the smells around me.

4. Ask for guidance and listen for answers. Some say when
    we pray, we ask for help, and when we meditate, we get
    it. I think that there is a fine line between prayer and
    meditation. When we are focusing on procuring our own
    peace, we learn to pray for guidance, not outcomes. In
    meditation, calming the mind and body and stepping out
    of chaos can allow us to see all the choices we have in
    front of us. Once we see our choices, the best choice often
    becomes clearer to us.

5. Practicing gratitude during a meditation can immediately
    improve your mood. There was a study that used an MRI
    to show the positive effects on brain function when some-
    one practiced gratitude, in addition to lowering their heart
    rate. Like with our controlled breathing, when we control
    our thoughts and focus on gratitude, we are causing a
    change in our physical state. Look at the power we actually
    have. Our thoughts can control our bodies! Actually, we
    already are aware of this. Think about how your body
    reacts when the phone rings or when you think about
    your child's behavior. That feeling in the pit of your stom-
    ach. The pounding in your head. Your jaw and shoulders
    may tighten. This is all a defensive response by your body
    because you told it that there was danger ahead. Take that
    same superpower and use it for good. Focus on gratitude.

SURRENDER

Sometimes it's not the times you fight but the times you surrender
that win the war. We've talked a lot about radical acceptance. In
order to find meaningful solutions, we have to be able to accept

what is out of our control so that we can focus on what we can control. Sometimes this means coming to terms with some very painful realities, like being unable to save our child. That doesn't mean our child can't be saved, and as we've seen, we can learn healthy ways to support our child, but ultimately, we are not the ones who can save them. They must save themselves. There are people who have been through what they are going through who may be able to help them figure out a solution better than we can. There are medical professionals who can help them as well. As parents, we are the least qualified to help them. Even for parents who have battled addiction themselves, if we had the power, our kids would be fixed by now. So, once we accept it, how do we come to peace with it? We surrender.

I placed surrender here in the book instead of following the section on Radical Acceptance for a reason. The first part of this book deals with addiction, and the second part of this book deals with moving forward with our lives. When I say that we need to surrender, I'm not talking about surrendering to the enemy, addiction. I'm not talking about giving up either. I'm talking about surrendering not just by acceptance but also with trust. We surrender and trust that God, the universe, however you want to identify it, something bigger than us, will handle it from here. And once again the importance of our belief system comes in. If we believe the universe is uncaring or hostile, then it will feel like just giving up or surrendering to the enemy. When we trust that the world is on our side, then we can experience a surge of release when we surrender. We can feel liberated. We become unburdened by releasing responsibility for things over which we have no power and knowing that we will be able to figure out a way to be okay regardless of how things turn out.

When we surrender in the spiritual sense, when we surrender to a trusted power greater than ourselves, we get more than release and relief. We also become empowered. We start to get a clearer picture of our own potential and our role in the universe. When all of that energy is freed, released if you will, we now have the opportunity to use it in a more helpful way. We can use our power in ways that it actually works. We can set up a system where we no longer exhaust ourselves by investing our energy in things where we have no control over the outcome. We begin to invest energy in ourselves and we can control the return on those investments. We surrender not only what we can't control, but we also surrender to the fact that there is so much we can control. We can change how we experience the world. We get to decide how we show up in our own lives. We get to take charge of how we are thinking on the inside and how we are behaving on the outside. We discover our superpowers.

There is a great story in one of the Al-Anon books. It tells the story of a woman driving to a liquor store after getting a call that her husband's tab had to be paid. She was across a four-lane street and saw her husband stumble into traffic. She couldn't do anything and watched as some stranger pulled her husband to safety. It was at that moment that she realized that it didn't have to be her to save him every time. She could let the world take over, just as it had. She went to the store and paid the tab and told the shopkeeper that she would never pay another tab so if he sold booze to her husband, it was his loss. That's surrender.

My favorite visual is this: picture wrapping your child in a warm cozy blanket in their favorite color and gently handing them over to the loving arms of the universe. Tell them how much you love them and how much you hope they get better. Promise them that you will do whatever you have to in order to become stronger yourself and learn the best ways you may be able to help them. Ask the universe to care for them lovingly and give them a kiss. Then keep your promise by getting to work on yourself.

LET'S GET TO WORK:
TAKING ACTION

"Committing to one small action can have profound results."

I would think that if you're reading this book, your life is feeling a bit war-torn. Your life has been hijacked by an enemy that has taken over your child's mind and body and has consumed you in the process. The chaos has become so normal that you may not even recognize it as such, and you feel like you're moving from one crisis to the next. In trying to fix your child, you have lost control over your own life. I get it. I was there. And I've escaped the spiral of chaos and crisis one gateway behavior at a time.

When my son was in the throes of active use, I stopped everything. I stopped working. I left a relationship. I stopped seeing friends. I couldn't focus on anything pleasant or productive. I stopped taking care of myself almost completely. When he decided to get help and left my home, I was no less of a wreck than when he was there. The chaos of my life had taken on a life of its own and it no longer just related to him. I had become a person who operated from a state of fear and crisis and continued to cause my own chaos by not tending to my own life. Much like I had to allow my son to fix himself, I needed to take responsibility and fix myself.

The best way to tackle chaos is by instilling order, so I started to get some order back in my life. But remember, by then, the chaos was coming from my own head, not things happening around me. I returned to work which was helpful in building some structure into my schedule, but the real work had to be done by me, concerning me. It started with a simple morning routine. I pulled out all those books I had purchased at my Al-Anon meetings and started reading from the daily readers every morning. It took less than five minutes to read a short page out of each. I would get up and make a cup of coffee, eagerly awaiting the calm of sitting on my couch, books by my side, coffee in hand. I read the daily page of each of those books like they had the elixir for life in them. I also signed up with two different places to receive a recovery-related quote each day, and I remember how I clung to those quotes like a lifeline on a ship. One would come by email by 8:00 a.m. and the other by text closer to 9:00 a.m. I would clutch my phone waiting with bated breath for words of wisdom that would somehow save me from the life I was living and show me a better way. It was that dramatic a time for me.

What I didn't realize at the time was that those little reading habits that I was developing were shifting my whole inner thought process. I was breaking the habit of waking up with dread and instead gave myself something to look forward to. I replaced worry with something that made me feel hopeful and calm. Doing these readings saved me, not just through their words, but the ritual of reading them restored order to my morning, and as my mornings began to have more order and purpose, my whole days started to go better.

During this time, I was also attending Al-Anon and parent support groups and my friends from these meetings and I would send each other texts about the readings. We would talk about what stood out for us or how it was exactly what we needed to hear that day. This fellowship that I was developing with other people who understood what I was going through was invaluable. I joke about how I used to say, "I'm not a group person," and now I run them. Building a support system is so helpful when we are facing these kinds of challenges. Hearing what has and has not worked for other people can give us new perspectives on how to proceed with our own decisions. Seeing people who experienced what I had and lived to tell and could laugh and seemed happy offered me a ton of hope. I also saw some people who were not doing as well and were stuck in the pain and misery. I was motivated to do the work on myself so I didn't end up stuck like them. I saw so many amazing parents who I looked at and thought, "There's no way this is their fault." The more I did that, the more I came to believe that maybe it wasn't my fault either.

Below I will discuss things that you can do on a daily basis to hone your skills with the tools we've discussed. If you incorporate even a fraction of these suggestions into your daily routine, I know you will experience huge shifts in how you're thinking and responding to your world. Instead of searching for answers, you'll realize that they will start to come to you because you will be clearing your mind enough to see what's already in front of you and inside of you. You'll feel yourself stepping out of the chaos and confusion and waking up with a renewed sense of peace and purpose and going to bed with a sense of repose instead of a simple relief that you got through the day. These practices are vital, and I cannot stress enough how important it is to build a support network as well. You cannot do this alone, nor should you. We only know what we know. We need others to see our blind spots. Surrounding yourself with caring people who understand is crucial. Even my one-on-one clients attend my parent support groups and sometimes other groups as well. I strongly encourage you to find a meeting. It can be Al-Anon or Nar-Anon or any other support group for parents or relatives of addicts. There are NAMI meetings if mental health is the stronger underlying issue. Either way, find a tribe. Even if it's just one or two other people that get it and want more from their lives, that's better than going it alone. When talking about our distorted thinking that brings chaos to our lives, there's a well-used saying: "My head is a dangerous neighborhood, and I shouldn't go there alone." There is safety in numbers. So let's get to work! To tackle the day, let's start at the beginning.

MORNING ROUTINE

"Win the morning, win the day." —*Tim Ferris*

I used to tease my late husband about his morning routine. I would say "You're the only person I know who, despite getting married and having four kids, still has the same morning routine you had in high school." It was a healthy morning routine; I just couldn't comprehend how he remained so disciplined with it and how it never got interrupted with all changes in his life. In one way, I respected it, and in another way, it annoyed the hell out of me. Looking back thirty years later, I appreciate it more. My late husband understood self-care and he was calm and peaceful in the morning. I, as a typical mother/martyr, sacrificed everything to accommodate him and then to accommodate each additional child as they came along. I can guarantee you I was probably brushing my teeth in the shower, trying to multitask as best I could. Maximizing time efficiency doesn't always breed self-care and calm. One thing my husband used to do was come to me after he tied his tie and have me put down his collar. It was cute when we were newlyweds, but by child four, it was really annoying and I told him as much, with very little finesse, one particularly stressful morning. As I'm writing this, I look back fondly on that patient man and at that stressed-out version of me. I've come a long way. I am a very different person than I was back then and even more different than I was just a couple of years ago when my son was in the throes of his addiction and I was in the throes of my own chaos. I say with all confidence that the most defining element of recovering my life was developing a morning routine.

As a child, my parents were fairly hands-off and I didn't have a lot of self-discipline, which basically meant I was always late for school, church, and just about everything else. When my children started playing school at home, my oldest started the game by saying, "Hurry up, we're late!" As parents, we are constantly teaching them, whether we realize it or not. They learn from watching us, so we better watch what we're showing them.

During my whole adult life, my morning had never been dictated by me. When I got married it was dictated by what my husband or cats needed. As I had children, their needs were added to my morning routine. I wasn't even aware that I had needs. Every few months my dad would come over to babysit and my husband and I would spend a night at a hotel and joke that as much as we loved getting up with the kids and making four chocolate milks, it was really nice to have a morning where we didn't have to. It's easy to get lost in the business of child-rearing. The natural progression is that they grow up and take on more and more of their own responsibilities, allowing us more time for ourselves. Things like waking them up and getting them dressed become their responsibilities and we may actually be able to have that cup of coffee. When that natural progression gets interrupted by addiction and mental health issues, we often don't get the chance to pass the torch of responsibility onto them. Beginning to take ownership of how our day goes, starting at the beginning of the day, helps to start putting us back in charge of our lives.

When our kids are small, it may seem hard to maintain a morning routine, but as our kids get older, it should become easier. The problem is that often, we've gotten so used to not having one that we don't realize we need it. Establishing a morning routine focused on Soul-Care, how you want to feel during the day, and how you want to feel at the end of the day is crucial to your recovery, peace, and growth. It will help you center yourself and set you on the path to making healthy gateway decisions that will carry you throughout the day, so that instead of a sense of relief at the end of the day, you will feel contentment. You'll begin to feel at home in your own life.

So how do you establish a morning routine when you're in crisis? You do it the same way you do everything else—one small step at a time. One gateway decision at a time. First, we have to establish what it is we really want. What does not being in crisis feel like? What do we want our lives to feel like? Do we want peace? Do we want adventure and excitement? Do we want to feel safe? Do we just not want to feel anything?

We can't get what we want if we don't know what we want. Even though our child may be suffering, we can still consider what we would like our lives to look and feel like. Our feeling good will never make our child feel worse. If anything, we are setting an example of how to get one's life back. We are modeling behavior. We need to really consider what we want in order to figure out what we need to do to get it.

You can start this way. Make a list of all the positive emotions you can think of that you would like to feel. Remember, this is right now. As we start to heal and recover, our answers might change. Don't judge your answers. Just go with your gut and identify a way you want to feel. Sometimes it's easier to know what you don't want than to identify what you do want, so if you have to, start there. List all the feelings you have during the day that you don't want to feel anymore. Again, don't judge your answers. Don't feel guilty if you have negative feelings toward people, especially your child. Feelings are never wrong. There are times when certain feelings aren't useful, and we'll get into that later, but for now, list all that you want and all you don't want. When my clients make these lists, the first list is usually much shorter than the second. It's hard to think about what you want when you have so little of it. Peace and calm are usually at the top, if not the only things on the list. When it comes to things they don't want to feel, the list grows more easily. They don't want to feel stressed, angry, sad, anxious, fearful, worried all the time (same as fear), resentful, and so on. Can you relate?

After you've made your one or two lists, pull out two or three of the positive emotions and decide to focus on those. You are going to decide that you will begin to fill your days with those emotions. How do you do this? By paying attention to all the decisions you're making during the day and intentionally choosing gateway decisions that lead to those feelings, you will begin to feel those feelings. First, I suggest writing down your intention for the day. It can be a word like *calm* or a phrase like *worry less*. I usually advise my clients to write it on a post-it and put it where they will see it multiple times during the day. You can put it on multiple post-its around your house or office. And don't worry about people seeing it. No one judges people for working on themselves, and if they do, forget about them. I had three words on my refrigerator one day and all my son's college friends came over and one of the guys asked, "Are those your inspiration words?" I said, "Yes, as a matter of fact, they are." He said, "Cool," and walked away. I was a little embarrassed and then I wondered why I should be embarrassed. Working on ourselves can feel very vulnerable. Looking at your life and admitting it needs to change is also admitting to it being a little messed up and that could mean admitting that you're a little messed up and that's vulnerable. It's okay. Trying new things can be scary. Stepping out of your comfort zone can be scary. Making changes can be scary. Just remember, you're not alone; we can all be scared together. Bravery isn't not being scared; it's doing what scares you even though you're scared.

ELEMENTS OF A MORNING ROUTINE

Once we begin to establish how we want to feel, and how we don't want to feel, we can start building our habits around practices that will lead to positive feelings. Although your morning routine will be tailored for you by you, there are some elements and practices that are objectively extremely helpful in helping you claim your day and go out into the world with intention.

START YOU DAY UNPLUGGED:
NO PHONE, NO EMAILS, NO NEWS

My coach once told me, "Do not consume until you create." That was her way of saying, "Don't pick up your cell phone or check your emails until you've set intentions for the day." The problem is when we check text messages, emails, news, or social media we are allowing someone else to command our day. Our mood is immediately affected by what we see or read first. Even if it puts us in a good mood, like a cute picture on Instagram, we are still relinquishing control over the direction of our thoughts.

We've all read articles about the dangers of our society's addiction to information and screens. We are never turned off. When we have a child in trouble, our phones begin to feel like our lifelines when, in fact, they just cause us to constantly search for information that makes no difference in the outcome of our children but just causes us to worry constantly. I was working with a client one day and had her pull out her phone and turn off the tracker she had on her son's phone. It gave her no valuable information. Her knowing where he was didn't change what he was doing, and it was making her obsessed by checking it constantly. She knew it was driving her crazy. She also knew that if she actually needed to, she could turn it back on. She felt a great sense of relief and freedom when she did it. Texting a child first thing in the morning to see if they're alive is one of the most toxic habits for parents.

It causes nothing but misery for the parent and makes no difference in the well-being of their child. Don't pick up your phone until you've completed your routine.

I'm writing this book during year two of the Covid pandemic. The constant flow of repeated information was incredibly unhealthy for so many. Little of the information was actually helpful. The conflicting information instilled more and more fear, and I am experiencing first-hand the damage done to so many clients from information overload and over-exposure to fear and tragedy. Most news reported is negative. If you start your day off with negativity it's going to be much harder to claim all those nice emotions as you go through the day. Don't turn on the news until you've done your routine if you have to turn it on at all.

No emails are so regularly urgent that they must be answered the moment you wake up, yet we all have to resist the urge to check our emails first thing in the morning. If you do have emails to respond to, you will be better off responding after you've finished your morning routine and your mind is clearer. Early morning email responses are often reactions. We want to avoid reacting and practice responding. The emails can wait; it's as simple as that.

The gateway decision here is the simple decision to pick up your phone or not. Some experts suggest charging your phone in a different room so you're not tempted to pick it up. You can turn it off at night so you can't look at it until it turns on, which could give you that extra moment to decide not to look at it. You can take some of the apps off your phone so that you need your computer to look at them and it eliminates the opportunity to grab your phone while your head is still on the pillow. Many of my clients have gone back to old-fashioned alarm clocks instead of using their phone alarms because once the phone is in their hand, the urge is too strong to check it. I encourage you to consider what you can do to break the habit of checking your phone first thing. Try a few things and find what works for you and stick to it.

It's not easy. Trust me, I know! My daughter and her husband went overseas for a few months, which meant my baby grandson went too. Years before, I had broken my habit of checking my phone before I got out of bed. All of a sudden, I started checking my phone because I would wake up to pictures of my grandson. That sounds lovely and healthy; what could go wrong? Even after all my years of doing this work, I was amazed at how much could go wrong so quickly. Once the phone was in my hand, I'd coo over pictures of the baby, and then I'd open Instagram. Instead of petting my three dogs lying next to me, I'd scroll my feed, which was filled with dogs that looked exactly like mine. Before I knew it, I was losing thirty minutes of my morning, awake in bed, looking at my phone. But it got worse, because when I finally did get up, I was unfocused. When I'm unfocused, my routine gets thrown off and when my routine is thrown off, my day is thrown off. In a matter of three weeks, my productivity tanked. And it was all because of the seemingly innocent decision to look at pictures of my grandson. That was the gateway decision I made. I had to train myself again to stop picking up my phone. I started making the pictures the reward for doing all the healthy things I knew I needed to do to start my day right.

The takeaway here should be that it's not easy, but you'll feel big changes with small steps, and if you have to course-correct, then do it. Start setting a goal to delay screen time a little each day until you're not picking up your phone, turning on the news, or opening your laptop until you know you have claimed your day.

OWN YOUR SECOND THOUGHT

We talked about waking up with dread and fear. We can't control our first thought in the morning, but we can control our second. It's not easy, but this is all about building new habits. We know it's hard, but it's doable and it's easier when you have a plan.

If you usually wake up filled with angst, for now, accept that as a fact. Tomorrow you will wake up stressed and worried. Okay, so what are you going to do about it?

A few years ago, it feels like a lifetime ago, I was at that job that was sucking my soul out. I was so miserable. The thing was, my life was great, but my job sucked. I would wake up in the morning with the same angst I had as if I was sitting in my office, except I was actually in my lovely bed surrounded by my dogs who were open to belly rubs. I literally had to force myself to roll over and pet my dogs. When I say "force myself," I mean the weight of the worry and angst was like sandbags on my body and I felt physically immobilized. Can you relate?

Meanwhile, I had my dogs, a huge source of comfort and relief twelve inches away, just waiting for me to acknowledge them. I trained myself so that when I woke up and started thinking about the office, I immediately rolled over and petted the dogs. The moment my hand hit their soft fur, my attitude changed. Even though I knew I would feel better, it was still really hard to do at first. I wished I had had these tools when I was waking up thinking about my son.

You deserve to be happy. You deserve to have peace. Although my dogs offered me comfort and helped my second thought be more positive, I added something else to my "still-in-bed routine" to enhance those second thoughts. I have a book of blessings by John O'Donoghue. He has a short morning blessing that basically says, "Thank you for letting me wake up and I look forward to whatever this day brings." I say this little blessing as I pet my dogs and a wave of peace washes over me. When I practice this little ritual before I even get out of bed, instead of grabbing my phone or taking a tumble down the rabbit hole, I claim my day before I even start my morning routine. My still-in-bed routine lights my soul and lightens my burdens so I can move forward, filled with positivity and possibility.

Start small. At first, you may go down the rabbit hole of negative thoughts. At least you'll be aware of it and aware that you do have a choice. Be aware that you can take control. Decide on your gateway decision. When I wake up feeling anxious, I will _____ [fill in the blank]. It can be anything that works for you. Cuddle your pet, say a prayer, recite a poem, sing your favorite song, jump out of bed before the second thought comes. Just keep reminding yourself that your mood is a choice and that your thoughts don't get to decide it, you get to decide.

DAILY READINGS

One of the best ways to get out of your own head is to get into someone else's. Actually, there's been a lot said already about the dangers of that, focusing on others instead of focusing on yourself. Here is an example of when allowing yourself to focus on someone else can be a healthy thing. There are millions of inspiring and motivational books in publication. Some are daily readers, some are spiritual guides, and some are memoirs of incredible people. Seek them out, take the ones that resonate with you, and incorporate them into your morning routine. Inspiration is not a one-and-done. It needs to constantly be fueled and nurtured. Change is the result of persistent and consistent gateway decisions. The biggest breakthrough is wasted if persistent action isn't taken to make the change a habit. We need to allow ourselves to be inspired on a daily basis, and when we start by adding inspiration to our morning routines, we set ourselves up to be inspired throughout our day.

Al-Anon daily readers are a great place to start, especially early on in our own recovery. They help us keep the disease in its proper perspective in our lives and give us insight into changes we can make in ourselves. As I've said before, improving how we relate to our addicted children and their disease is only part of the message of this book. Because of this, I encourage you to also find books that have nothing to do with addiction. Part of putting addiction in its proper perspective is to spend most of our time not thinking about it. Find books that inspire you and interest you. Novels are great for relaxation and entertainment, but they don't help with personal growth. There are thousands of other books on personal growth. They are focused on us helping ourselves find peace, joy, and happiness and creating lives we love. When I pose the idea of finding peace and joy to my clients, they ask me how. There are a million ways and hundreds of books to help you find what works for you. Commit to reading three pages each morning. If the book is worth it, you'll find inspiration in three pages per day. Remember, the goal here is gateway habits to build morning routines that become second nature. You want to feel so good after your morning routine that you won't want to miss it, ever. When the 7:00 a.m. call comes in from your addicted child or your annoying brother, you won't be tempted to answer it right away because you will be in such a state of peace that you won't be tempted to interrupt it. This is the end goal.

If our addicted child goes into recovery, they are told to create a life beyond their wildest dreams, a life so good they would never risk it by using again. I say the same of us as parents. We have to create a life that is so peaceful and joyful, where we feel so empowered that we would never risk it by falling back into our old ways of trying to fix everyone and control things that don't belong to us. We don't want to wake up with angst and constantly worry. My clients always say, "I just want peace." I get it; peace is part of it. I encourage them to find joy as well. Joy is personal. For me, joy includes a bit of adventure. I love to travel and explore. For some of my clients, it's rediscovering things they loved that they stopped doing: painting, knitting, exercising, or reading for pleasure. For others, they just want to enjoy retirement without drama and chaos. We each get to choose.

Our child's addiction made our lives very small. We gave up pleasure after pleasure without realizing it. When we think about our child, we find that we went from dreams and hopes for a great life to sometimes just hoping they stay alive. When we look closely enough, we find that the same has happened to our expectations for our own lives. We end up in survival mode and the thought of having a bigger, more fulfilling life seems incomprehensible. Be inspired by others who have made changes in their lives. You don't have to reinvent the wheel. People change their lives all the time; luckily, so many of them have written about it. For me, John O'Donohue's books and Victoria Castle's "The Trance of Scarcity" are my go-to books. In Al-Anon we often say when you're looking for a sponsor, find someone who has what you want and then do what they did to get it. Find someone that inspires you and read their story, a few pages a day, to incorporate inspiration into your morning routine and to remind you that it is totally possible for your life to get better if you make one positive gateway decision at a time.

MEDITATION

Earlier in this book we talked about meditation when we talked about faith and spirituality and the significance of them in our recovery. If we don't believe in the possibility for our lives to get better, then why would we even try? And notice I didn't say we have to believe that our lives will get better. We simply have to start to allow for the possibility that they may be able to get better, in order to start making those gateway decisions toward peace and joy. The belief will come from the doing. As we make slight changes and start to feel the effect of those changes, we will eventually come to believe. Making meditation part of your morning routine will allow you to begin the day being present, thinking only of that day, not what happened yesterday and not what may happen later. The only truth is in the moment, so start your day there.

I have found meditation to be one of those practices where I really have to convince my clients that there is a possibility that meditation may help them, and they should try it. The thought of quieting the mind in the midst of the chaos of addiction is hard to imagine. Be gentle. The goal is not to silence the mind. The goal is to quiet it, a little more each day, one moment at a time. We are building habits here. Collecting tools that will help us lead better lives. When we buy a power tool, first we purchase it, then we use it the first time, then we keep using it until we get really good at using it. Sometimes we read the instructions, and that helps, and sometimes we wing it and figure it out through trial and error. Either way, the point is that honing our skills takes time and practice. Learning how to meditate in a way that serves you best will take time and practice as well. When you make it part of your daily routine, and you practice it a little bit each day, you will hone your skills and reap the benefits. Like other practices that result in a better quality of life with more peace and joy, you will begin to rely on it so much that you won't want to miss it and you won't relinquish your meditation time to unhealthier things.

You can start small. Before your daily readings, take five deep slow breaths with your eyes closed. Just presence yourself. Where are your hands? What does your body feel? What do you smell? What do you hear? Is there a taste in your mouth? When I work with a client, and even at the beginning of my support groups, I hold sixty-nine seconds of silence—deep breathing, eyes closed—before we start. I sometimes open my eyes to gauge the level of comfort in the others. Some of the discomfort I observe reminds me of the Alanis Morrissette song, "All I Really Want." In it she asks why we're so scared of silence, then offers a quiet beat. She then lists all the stressful things we probably thought about during it.

Sitting quietly with ourselves can be challenging and, if we dig deep, very scary. Initially we may be scared because we can anticipate our minds going to dark places that we're used to, worst-case scenarios about our child's addiction. It can be even more terrifying if we start to think that our minds may go to the dark places deep inside of us that we haven't yet explored. We often fear exploring those deep hidden fears and insecurities that make us who we are and prevent us from being who we want to be.

When I'm working with a client and dealing with meditation resistance, I like to start small and on a very positive note. Visualization can be a great way to meditate when you're starting out. I have them think about a really happy memory. I make sure they smile. I encourage them to remember it in the most specific detail they can. What colors do they remember? What did it smell like? What was the temperature in the air? What did it feel like? Happy? Peaceful? Exciting? What were the specific sensations in their body at the time? Do this for just a minute or two, before your mind has time to wander. You can even set a timer for two minutes. When you open your eyes, notice how you feel. Are you still smiling? Are your shoulders relaxed? Is there lightning in your chest and body? Hopefully the answers are yes. Even my most resistant clients find that when they meditate in the morning, their day goes better. One of my clients said that now he won't start his day without meditating. Sometimes he just has to squeeze it into five quiet minutes in the shower, but no matter what, he won't skip it.

I've said that meditation is about being present. Focusing on a happy memory can actually change your physical and emotional state. There is power in our thoughts. We often accept the power of negative thinking more easily than we accept the power of positive thinking. We all know that if we focus on worry and negativity, our emotional state becomes unpleasant and our whole body tenses. And it follows that if we focus on positive things, we will feel more positive and our body will relax! If we focus on the present moment and our immediate surroundings, we can feel peace because, when we are focusing on the moment, we are creating our own peace. We are not worrying about the future or ruminating about the past. We have the power to create our own peace, even if we have to do it moment by moment and even if there isn't a lot of peace around us. When we enter the present moment, we will find peace.

Practice silence. Practice focus. Focus on your breath, focus on a mantra or a prayer, and use essential oils to follow your breath through your lungs. Say the Hail Mary ten times. Try it all and stick with what works for you. Meditation is the tool; these suggestions are various ways to practice our skills so we get good at using the tool. Eventually our skills will be honed and we will feel off if we miss our meditation. Missing my morning meditation costs me hours in lost productivity because I start the day unfocused. I end up vulnerable to the influences and distractions of everything going on around me. Taking the time to quiet my mind and focus on my intentions makes my whole day more efficient and more productive. It helps me focus on what I want for my day instead of allowing negative thoughts to rule the day.

ON TO PAPER AND OUT OF YOUR MIND

Incorporating writing into your morning routine serves a very important purpose. It can allow you to vent and dump a lot of negative thoughts onto the page where you can begin to see them for the stories they are. I sometimes instruct my clients to write out their absolute worst-case scenario for life, which is often the current story they're telling themselves, then we start to dissect it to determine its truth and its value. From there, we can come up with a number of other possible stories they can tell themselves that can serve them better. One of the most common stories, for instance, is that self-care is selfish and focusing on yourself is unacceptable when your child is suffering. I help them reframe that story to a more useful one. *If I take care of myself, I will be strong enough to help others. If I don't take care of myself, I won't be.* When you do this at the start of the day, you can enter the day with a lot less baggage and when you find yourself telling yourself these distorted stories, you'll be able to recognize them for what they are and reframe them as you go along. You won't fix what you don't realize is broken and journaling can help you identify where the fractures in your thinking are.

I used to fear that writing down bad thoughts would somehow make them more real. I have actually found the opposite to be true. Writing them down puts them into perspective and often deflates their power over my mood and prevents them from causing a downward spiral of catastrophizing. I remember times when I would get mad at my husband. I'd work myself up in my own head and find the perfect things to say to get my point across and usually, to convince him that he had done something wrong. More often than not, after ruminating on it for God knows how long, the moment the words left my mouth, I realized they didn't sound nearly as good as they had in my head and I regretted saying them. Like those text messages we've all sent at some point. For me, dumping these thoughts onto pages no one will see and I will likely never look at again has the same effect without the negative consequences. Once I see things written, I can better evaluate whether they're accurate or useful or just me telling myself false stories.

In *The Artist's Way*, Julia Cameron teaches a practice of daily pages to free up creative blocks. She suggests taking a pen to paper and writing three pages of free thought, a simple stream of consciousness, each morning to clear your headspace. She says that some of her students do these pages on a yellow pad, then stuff them into an envelope and toss them away each month.

Hers isn't a creative writing assignment or to-do list. It's a brain dump of all the negative thoughts that might hold you back during the day. You can use this to dump all the thoughts and worries and just leave them on the pages. It's more about getting rid of stuff than contemplating it, and when our kids are struggling, we have a lot to get rid of.

When I'm working with clients, I also encourage them to journal about what they want their life to look and feel like. A huge part of recovery is learning to live with intention; not just responding better to the world around us, but changing the world around us through our perception and our actions. We'll never get what we want if we don't know what we want, and the chaos caused by addiction strips us of the energy to focus on our own joy. A lack of crisis is not the same as peace and learning how to not allow our child's addiction to destroy us is not the same as us actually feeling joy. It's easy to identify how we don't want to feel. Spending time focusing on how we do want to feel allows us to make an action plan on how to achieve it. Then we can look at our life and see which thoughts and behaviors are preventing us from feeling that way. Once we have clarity, we can take action. Journaling is a great way to get this clarity.

INTENTION SETTING

Intention setting is another way to take back control of your life and empower yourself for the day. When I refer to setting an intention, I'm simply referring to deciding how you want your day to feel and then committing to making decisions that will most likely result in those feelings. Early on, the intention may be that you'll worry less that day. That will mean that you will be conscious of when you begin to worry and will do something to occupy your mind with something either more pleasurable or more productive, or both. It may also mean that you agree to pull out your journal when you start to worry and brain dump all the fears, then close your journal and leave the fears behind. Intention setting is a desire plus a plan to achieve that desirable outcome. It's simple but can have a huge impact on your mindset for the day. Think of your mind like a scale. Scales are tested and calibrated to make sure that when a known weight, say 2g, is placed on it, it actually reads 2g. After so many times weighing things, a scale has to be recalibrated. Our minds are weighed down by thousands of thoughts throughout the day. Some say that the average human has 6,200 thoughts per day. After so many thoughts, it makes sense that our minds would need to be recalibrated during the day. An intention is like a calibration weight, that known weight used to test a scale. During our morning routine, we decide what we want to focus on, and that becomes our calibration weight. Throughout the day we keep checking in with ourselves to make sure we're staying somewhat focused on our intention, and if we are not, then we get to recalibrate our thinking to focus on our intention.

Setting an intention can be simple. You can pick a word or a phrase that expresses how you want to behave or feel for the rest of that day. It's different from a motivational quote, which can be focused on something you want to accomplish that day. When setting an intention, you have to think about what you want your day to feel like or what kind of person you want to be.

My client Corinna loved this idea, but she didn't think she would be able to keep an intention in mind all day. Instead of a phrase or an intention, she picked one word and wrote it on post-its all over her house and office. For example, one morning she chose the word *calm*. Every time she saw the word, she would check in with herself to see if she was really feeling calm. It took less than two weeks for her to go from a single word to whole phrases, like *today I will practice gratitude in everything I do*. When she would see that phrase during the day, she would check in and make a note of something she was grateful for.

The most vital role I play in coaching my clients is to help them recognize the stories they tell themselves and how belief in those stories affects their decision-making. We all tell ourselves stories. Most of the time we don't realize we're doing it, but it is human nature to tell stories. Many of these stories lead to us believing things that are simply not objectively true. Many lead to limiting beliefs that prevent us from doing things that will lead us to happier and healthier lives. Our stories make us who we are because we make behavioral decisions based on what we believe to be true or not and, as we said earlier, our behaviors define us. When a client talks about their life in a negative, hopeless way, I help them recognize that they are telling themselves stories usually based on their deepest fears or insecurities and that these stories are not reality. Or, at least, they're not the only available reality. Even if they are really struggling at the moment, the story shouldn't be that because they are struggling now, they will struggle forever. Remember, we can direct our thoughts. We can course-correct all day long if we have to in order to keep our thoughts moving in a direction that propels us forward toward a peaceful and joyful life.

Intentions help remind us that we spend the day telling ourselves stories without realizing it. When we can return to the intention we set early in the day, we remind ourselves to retell the story, and this time, make it work for us. You may be having a crappy day, but when you are reminded that you decided to practice gratitude, you begin to tell yourself the story that there are many things to be grateful for and that a few crappy things don't make your entire day or your entire life crappy. If we set the intention to take things less personally, when we find ourselves asking, "Why is this happening to me?" or getting upset at something a stranger did, we can remind ourselves of our intention and remember that whatever it was didn't happen to us, it simply happened and whatever that stranger did, they simply did; you were a random bystander, it wasn't personal. We are what we focus on. If we focus on the negative stuff, we will be unhappy and give off negative energy. If we focus on the good stuff, we will be happier and give off positive energy. Our thoughts are very powerful; we have to remember that. They control who we are.

When I started setting intentions for the day, I would write them in my daily planner so that I would see them every time I checked my calendar. Sometimes I would post them on my fridge or my bathroom mirror to help remind me of them during the day. They became my daily mantra to gently remind myself to do better that day. They also allowed me to focus on one thing to change at one time. If I got stressed during the day, I would go back to that single intention to refocus and recalibrate. I didn't have to go through the list of all the things I needed to improve and make a decision every time I needed to redirect my energy. My decision for my focus was determined by my morning intention, and I knew that I didn't have to focus on anything but that one thing for that one day. It slowed me down so that I could breathe and be present.

Setting intentions helps us make gateway decisions that lead us to a peaceful, more fulfilling life. Corinna reported that one day she was feeling furious with her boss when she saw the word "pause" on her monitor. She said she wasn't happy to see it initially. Old habits die hard, but then she made that gateway decision to be true to her morning intention for the day. She took a couple of deep breaths and decided to wait until later that day, when she had calmed down, to look at why she was angry and see how much of it was a story in her head and what, if anything, she needed to do about it. Ah, the power of the pause, and the power of an intention. Later that day when she looked at the situation, she realized that she was taking her boss's words too personally and was able to address the issue she had brought up calmly and productively.

Intentions support the long-term effort to become a better you, a more empowered you, a you with a love of life and healthy boundaries. To be the kind of person you wish you were, calmer, kinder, happier, and more empowered in your life. The kind of person that understands the value of Soul Care and practices it without guilt, knowing that the more emotionally healthy you are, the better you can show up for everyone around you. You can take command of your life and protect your peace and joy.

Early on in your practice of this, if you are still in the throes of chaos, a simple word like *breathe* may be all you need to remind you to relax your shoulders and jaw, close your eyes, and breathe for a minute or two. Try it. As you build your morning routine, pick a word that represents a feeling or behavior that is a gateway to peace. Write it wherever you will see it multiple times during the day. Set a reminder on your phone for every hour to remind yourself to breathe or stay calm, whatever your word is.

This is also a great time to check in with your body. It's hard to calm the mind when the body is sending the brain messages of stress. Contracted muscles in your shoulders or neck, in your hands, or a clenched jaw all tell the brain that there is something wrong. They cause the brain to release stress hormones, particularly cortisol. If we want our minds to calm down, we need to tell our bodies to as well. When you think of your intention, pay attention to your body. Relax your jaw, drop your shoulders, and take a few deep breaths. Shake your arms to loosen up. Rub your hands together. Rubbing your hands together stimulates certain nerve endings that produce delta waves, which calm the brain. Remember, we want our bodies and our minds to both tell better stories, so when we check in with our thoughts, we should check in with our muscles too.

One final note on intentions: we've talked about practicing gratitude. Practicing compassion is equally as important. Gratitude focuses on ourselves; compassion is about our place in the world.

Particularly when dealing with difficult loved ones, like an addicted child, compassion can help us realize that hurt people hurt people and that most of the time, when someone is unkind or exhibiting unacceptable behavior, they are coming from their own place of pain. Compassion does not imply that we accept unacceptable behavior. Compassion allows us to respond with a positive emotional response, and when we respond with a positive response, we are increasing the positive energy around us. We feel better and more at peace when we respond with compassion. When we can attribute bad behavior to another person's pain, it becomes easier for us to not take it personally and tell ourselves stories that focus on us when it usually has little to do with us. When we take things less personally, we find it easier to let go of the negative emotions around both the other person and their behavior and any resentments that we may form around them. The opposite of compassion is often anger, which leads to us delivering negative energy to the world around us and makes it much harder for us to let go of resentments, resulting in the hurt perpetuating and exacerbating. In Al-Anon they say that resentments are like taking poison and expecting someone else to get sick. Don't punish yourself by holding onto things that cause you pain. It's like the thorn in your foot; you'd pull it out the moment you know it's there. Extract your resentments through compassion and ease your own pain. Practice Soul Care.

Consider adding compassion to your intention list. If you're on a crowded train, look around at the people and think of all the crap they're each dealing with. Take a deep breath and breathe out compassion, like a little random act of kindness and send a little hope that their crap gets better. Then check in with your body and see how you feel. I used to do this with my children when stuck in traffic on long car rides to Cape Cod. We would be on our way to the beach and other people were missing important stuff. Even worse, some people were in accidents. Traffic jams are a great place to realize that all those people in the cars around you are having a shared experience with different interpretations and consequences for sure, but from a compassion standpoint, no one expected to be sitting there instead of making progress to their destination. It's another great place to just sit in your car and breathe in love and breathe out compassion and say a little prayer that everyone in traffic with you feels a little more love that day. Then see how different you feel after you've said that. I often offer a small nod of understanding if I make eye contact with another stuck driver. I have never been met with anything other than a nod back and a hint of a smile. People need to be understood. They need to not feel alone. Random acts of compassion can go a long way in increasing positive energy and uplifting ourselves and the recipients of our compassion. A rising tide raises all boats. Be intentionally part of the good in the world.

WAYS TO COMBAT
WORRY AND STRESS
THROUGHOUT THE DAY

*"Worrying is like a rocking chair; it gives you something
to do but gets you nowhere."* —*Irma Bombeck*

It's hard to tell people not to worry when there is a real crisis in
their lives. The issue is not whether the worrying is justified but
rather, whether it's useful. Spoiler alert: it isn't. It's like guilt. It's
a waste of emotional bandwidth, and let's face it, most of us have
limited emotional bandwidth. People often confuse worry with
vigilance. "I have to worry because otherwise it won't get done."
"If I don't worry about it, no one will." "If I hadn't worried, I
wouldn't have known she was doing drugs." Worrying and vigilance are not the same. Knowing something is wrong and finding
out what it is, is action. Usually, worry stands on its own, like a
massive stone casting a weighted shadow that bears down on
our souls, blocks out any ray of light or hope, and leaves us too
heavily burdened to do anything. Action is empowering, worry is
depleting. The more we worry, the more worrying becomes one
of our baseline behaviors and we start to define ourselves by our
worrying. In come the stories we tell ourselves. "I am a worrier;
I can't help it; it's who I am." I can't count the number of times

parents have quoted this to me. I help them break it down and rephrase it. "I am not a worrier; sometimes I worry." "It's not that I can't help it; I have to change my understanding of it and develop better habits around my tendency to worry." "It's not who I am; it's what I sometimes do, and I am learning how to do it less often."

So how do we control our worrying? First, we have to understand why we worry, and the answer is not because we have something to worry about. Statistically, over 90 percent of things a person worries about never happen. That aside, when we have a child who is struggling or suffering, we can easily claim that we do, in fact, have something to worry about. Justified or not, it doesn't help the situation and it tortures the crap out of us. We worry because we come up with the worst possible outcome and then we treat it like it is reality. According to Oxford Languages, when we worry, we give way to anxiety and we allow our mind to dwell on troubles. Notice it says to give way and to allow. Those are both actions that indicate a person is making a choice and willingly choosing misery. Worrying is a choice, not a personality trait. It is a habit; and like any habit, it can be broken. And like any ingrained habit, changing it takes persistence and time. The good news is the rate of change of a habit depends on the frequency of the habit, so if you worry all the time, then you have all those opportunities to break the habit even faster than if you didn't worry often.

Breaking the habit of worrying involves a few things. First, we have to go back to radical acceptance. Whatever our biggest worries are, we have to look at each situation objectively. First, is it a truth or is it something that we are afraid might happen? If it is true, then we need to figure out how much control we actually have over it. If our biggest worry is our child's addiction, then we have to radically accept that we have no control over their addiction. That doesn't mean we don't have control over other aspects of the effects their addiction is having on our own lives. The opposite of worry is not peace. The opposite of worry is action. Worry is passive and results in us feeling powerless. Action allows us to step into our power. We cannot control our child's addiction, but we can take action to control how we respond to our child's addiction and how we care for ourselves as we are dealing with the challenges their disease presents us with. We need to take action to change how we are responding to the world, or we will never find peace. And when we do take action and change ourselves, we change our world.

I help my clients step out of worry and begin to regain power in their lives by taking action around their own behavior. A struggling child gives us a legitimate reason to be concerned, which can lead to the delusion that we can fix it. Worrying doesn't help us take action or make any improvement to the situation. When we can step out of worry, which we've already discussed causes panic, which puts us into crisis mode, which decreases our executive functioning and therefore our ability to make sound decisions, we become better able to see the situation for what it is and determine which actions, if any, we can take to help. If we determine that it is truly out of our control and there is nothing we can do to help, then we can take action to change how we are responding. When we stop worrying it doesn't mean that we stop caring. It doesn't mean we stop trying to support our child. It also doesn't mean that we stop being sad about it. It simply means that we are using our energy toward more productive endeavors that lead to inner peace instead of inner turmoil. And the more inner peace we have, the more everyone around us benefits.

When you find yourself worrying, try these practices. List all the things you are worried about. Look at the list and cross out all the things that you have no control over or that simply belong to someone else and, therefore, you have no control over. Then look at what's left. Are they real situations or are they things you fear?

If they are things you fear, check in with your body and tell your mind that they are not really happening and you don't have to be scared. Take deep, slow breaths and relax your body so that your mind gets the message. You can pull out your journal and brain dump. You can pull out your sensory box and reset. Move a muscle to change a thought. Get up and do something productive or pleasurable. Tell yourself a new story, one where you are enjoying the moment rather than catastrophizing about the worst-case scenario of what could happen in the future. If worry is your first thought, then own your second.

THE EVENING ROUTINE
AND SLEEPLESS NIGHTS

*"I love sleep. My life tends to fall apart when
I'm awake."* —*Ernest Hemingway*

It's ironic that when our lives are at their most stressful points
and we most need a good night's sleep, restful sleep eludes us.
When we are in a state of chaos and crisis, our mind is out of
sync with our bodies, and what our bodies need most, our minds
can't provide. We have to address sleep, how to get to sleep, and
what to do when we wake up in the middle of the night and our
thoughts are racing.

There are two phases to our day: our waking phase and sleeping phase. And we all know that without a good sleeping phase,
it's really hard to have a good waking phase and vice versa. So
how do we prepare for a good sleep phase? The same way we
prepare for a good waking phase: with a healthy routine to get
started and a plan to course-correct if it goes wrong. We need an
evening or bedtime routine that includes rituals that put us in a
relaxed state, and we need tools to help us get back to sleep if it
gets interrupted. The best way to protect our sleep is to drift off
with a calm and uncluttered mind.

UNPLUG EARLY AND SET UP RITUALS

One of the first suggestions for the morning routine is to unplug. Don't pick up your phone first thing in the morning. More and more studies are coming out showing the negative effects that screen time is having on our sleep as well. In addition to the light they emit that throws off our circadian rhythms and causes us to produce waking hormones like cortisol, when we're supposed to be producing calming hormones like melatonin to help us sleep, we also go into information overload when we are supposed to be calming our thoughts down. Stop the screen time as early as you can before bedtime. It's tempting, I know, but we're dealing with enough with our kids. It's ridiculous for us to make things any more difficult for ourselves. This is another example of self-focus and taking responsibility for our own behaviors. Look at what you're doing on your phone or computer. Here's an opportunity to assess your gateway decision. Are you looking at things that will lead you to a revolving door or things that will make you feel better and propel you forward in your positive thinking? If you are someone who is on their phone or computer up until bedtime, start to wean yourself off. Find something else to do that can put you into a state of mind that will encourage peaceful sleep. All of the spiritual practices we talked about earlier are perfect for evening routines as well. You can look at morning and evening routines on the whole as a spiritual practice. All of the habits we build and practices we put into place are for centering ourselves, shifting our focus to our own behavior, and making changes based on gateway decisions that lead us to happier, more peaceful, and fulfilling lives.

Building pleasant rituals into our evening routine is helpful in setting ourselves up for a good night's sleep and getting out from in front of our screens. Think about little indulgences that might give you something to look forward to in an evening routine. It may be a hot bath or a leisurely shower. It could be a skincare routine.

When was the last time you read a book by your favorite author or took the time to listen to your favorite music? Part of us getting our lives back is rediscovering what brings us joy. If we work all day and are on our phones all night, where is the time for joy? Ending our day by filling our souls with things that light us up is a great way to honor ourselves.

OWN YOUR LAST THOUGHT

We said earlier that we couldn't control our first thought, but we can control our second thought. Now it's time to tackle our last thought. When we go to sleep with negative thoughts, we fall asleep anxious. We don't sleep as well, and we increase the risk of waking up with negative thoughts. We need to be mindful of our focus as we try to fall asleep. This means we need to look at what we are reading and watching. Watching true crime shows is unlikely to destress and lead us to more positive thinking. Who is the last person you speak with before going to sleep? Do you feel like you have to check on the addict before you go to sleep? Is that helping you? Do you fall asleep thinking that tomorrow will be a good day or a bad day? This goes back to our basic belief system. If we can make the little gateway decision to fill our bedtime with positive emotions, we can increase our chance of a good sleep and be ready to start the next day on a better foot.

Our mind believes what we tell it. It doesn't judge whether it's good or bad or true or false. We create our own stories, and our mind takes them at face value. Going back to our somatic responses, our somatic state also affects our minds. If our bodies are tense, our brains will not relax, and sleep will not be peaceful. Between our minds and our bodies, we have to be aware of the stories we're telling ourselves. If we tell our minds that things are okay and we relax our bodies to show that things are okay, things will start to feel okay.

Have you ever seen those people who can remain incredibly calm under pressure? An athlete, someone in a car accident, or a mother when one of her kids gets hurt. Some people just have the ability to stay calm. I guarantee you that each of those people is having an inner dialogue, telling themselves that it will be okay. What "okay" looks like is not relevant. They know that getting caught up in the pressure will not allow them to think or perform at optimum. They calm their thoughts so that they can think clearly. You see athletes on the starter blocks taking deep breaths before the gun goes off. They are centering and calming themselves. The deep breaths allow them to relax their somatic state to help calm their minds. We need to work on positive stories and tell ourselves those positive stories through our thoughts, our words, and through the state of our bodies.

JOURNALING

Journaling in the evening or at bedtime is a great way to help you guide yourself to a more positive thought pattern. Here are some ideas to inspire your evening journaling. A brain dump is a great way to get rid of anything that may be bothering us by writing it down and getting it out of our heads. We can write about the good things that happened and do a gratitude and appreciation list of all the things that happened that day. We can do an inventory and celebrate any wins we had that day. No win is too small to mention.

You can use your journal to set your intention for the night and perhaps for the following day, or you can use the journal to tell yourself a story that you'll sleep peacefully that night, and if you do wake up, that you will be able to go back to sleep without great effort.

A great prompt is what one of my coaches calls a future pull; I'll call it a peace pull. We'll let ourselves be pulled into a peaceful place. Pretend you had a perfect night's sleep and write about what it feels like and how you feel in the morning after waking up from such a sleep. Imagine and write about how it feels to nap at the beach or some other place we may wish we were at the moment. You can use the writing to presence yourself and declutter your mind. Write about it as if you are experiencing it. List what you see, what you smell, what you hear, and what your body feels like. Is there a taste in your mouth? This might feel weird or uncomfortable at first, but the more we are able to imagine ourselves in a place of peace and joy, the more we can identify the emotions we would feel in such a place, the more we can alter our present state to feel those same emotions. Just think, when we worry about bad stuff, we make ourselves feel like it's real. When we peace pull, we're doing the same thing except we're doing it to bring us peace and joy rather than misery.

No matter what you journal about, make sure that it is positive and calming. The goal is to be able to sleep. The stimulating writings can be handled in the morning journaling. This is all about winding down and staying calm and positive.

WAKING UP IN THE MIDDLE OF THE NIGHT

We've all experienced waking up in the middle of the night consumed by stress and worry and we know the terrible effects it has on us mentally and physically. It's one of the most pressing issues I see with parents. They wake up in the middle of the night and their minds go from zero to 60, down the rabbit hole. A healthy evening and bedtime routine can help with this, as will all the practices we've learned, but I'll give you some tips you can start to use right away for those difficult sleepless nights to get some immediate relief. You are not alone in this.

I mentioned a sensory box when I first discussed our somatic state. If your thoughts are out of control in the middle of the night, it's a great time to turn to your sensory box. They say you should move a muscle to change a thought. A sensory box allows you to not only move a muscle but to introduce positive things into your immediate environment, interrupting your thought pattern and bringing you a little joy. Your box is filled with things that delight you and calm you. Use them! Study them closely. Notice how you feel when you touch, smell, or feel them. Put on that calming music that you picked out for just such an occasion. Have that little nibble of chocolate or get a cup of warm milk with cinnamon. Think back to childhood or maybe to when your children were small. What comfort was offered to the child afraid in the middle of the night? What do you wish had been offered? Be kind to yourself. What can you do to offer yourself comfort?

Having appropriate readings on hand can also help. You don't want to start reading a novel at 2:00 a.m., but if you have one of your recovery books or spiritual readings, you can use them to help you refocus your thinking on the positive possibilities instead of the negative ones. I say *possibilities* because, after all, our fears are just stories we tell ourselves. We talked about worry and how an overwhelming amount of the stuff we worry about never actually happens. When we work on our worry-reducing skills and see that these late nights are just filled with worry, we'll tell ourselves different stories. If we find ourselves ruminating, we can remind ourselves that right now, at that very moment, as we lie in bed, there is nothing at all we can do about it and, more importantly, whatever we are thinking about is not happening at that very moment. We are in the comfort of our own bed, and to the best of our knowledge, all is well, so why sacrifice that precious moment of calm by thinking of negative things? This is the respite we've hoped for all day; we can't waste it.

You can also try guided meditations if your thoughts are running amuck. The internet is teeming with soothing voices offering inspiring and positive affirmations and guidance. There are tons of apps for this as well. Look for them. Listen to a few and find some you like. Often these late nights can feel lonely; sometimes, hearing someone's voice can be a great comfort.

This isn't easy, and when we wake up in the middle of the night scared, it doesn't matter how old we are; we need comfort. My daughter did sleep training with my grandson when he was four months old. After one week, he was sleeping through the night. Although the training involved letting them cry, it focused on teaching the baby to self-soothe. It encouraged the parents to give the baby the chance and the space to learn how to calm themselves without intervention from the parents. Babies who can self-soothe sleep better and longer and, needless to say, so do the parents. Like these babies, we can learn how to self-soothe and reclaim our sleep. We don't have to fix the world to get relief. We just have to fix our thought patterns. It all comes down to our stories. All we need is already inside of us.

CULTIVATE JOY

"Choose joy."

Driving over the bridge the day my husband was killed, watching the smoke billowing toward the sky, I chose joy. I didn't feel joy at the time. I didn't feel joy for a very long time. But I decided that if it wasn't my time to die, then my goal was to live with joy and to teach my children how to have a joyful life even if bad things happen. In February of 2002, I took the kids to Captiva Island in Florida and brought two of my closest friends with me. These friends could do what I couldn't yet do: they brought joy. They could be fun when I couldn't be. I could be responsible, but I couldn't yet be joyful. Watching my children play and laugh and seem normal for that week was a huge comfort to me. I saw that it was possible. I have a picture of the five of us taken on the beach against the sunset on our last evening there. The picture sits on my dresser in a frame that states "Life is good." I look at that picture every day and I understand its significance. It was at the moment that that picture was taken that I knew that we would be okay. I didn't know how, but I knew we would be.

As I began to make my own way out of the smoke-filled front line of Patrick's war with drugs and alcohol, when that lightbulb went on and I realized what a trainwreck I had become, I once again chose joy. I didn't know how I was going to find joy again, but I knew that it was possible, and I knew that I wanted to. Much like before, surrounded by people who could do what I couldn't yet, I rediscovered joy.

Find what lights you up and do a lot of it. If you can't come up with something, then try new things. Start small. Try a book by a new author, a paint-by-number, or a trip to a great chocolate shop. Pick up the instrument you used to love playing or blast the music you listened to in high school. Take a walk and notice things that make you smile. Joy is a way of being. It's a mindset that allows you to be okay even when the world goes to hell around you. It's not selfish. It's quite the opposite. Joy is what allows you to bring your best self to the world and to spread love and positivity. It's what allows you to live life on life's terms and have true inner peace. It's what I believe we were born for. For your own sake and the sake of all those around you, I invite you to choose joy.

MY HOPE FOR YOU, DEAR READER

This book is a labor of love, an offer of hope, and, I hope, a guiding light. I lived through my nightmares, and the lessons I've learned and shared with you have allowed me to build a life beyond my wildest dreams. I hold the same hope for you. I hope that you recognize the amazing gift you are to the world and that you deserve to have the life of your dreams, even if others you love don't. I hope that you can believe that you were meant for more than a life of chaos and fear. And as you start to build your joy-filled life, I hope you reach out and help someone else who is struggling.

Heal the hole in your soul the way you wish you could fix your child's. Take all of that love and give it to yourself as well. Love is like sunshine; there's enough for everyone. Step out of the shadow of this dreaded condition and soak up the sun. Nurture yourself. Pamper yourself. Be kind and compassionate to yourself.

Tell yourself wonderful stories. Set boundaries to protect yourself. Identify your needs and make sure they are met. Cultivate joy in your life.

Reclaim your power in your life and from that powerful position you can do great things. You will make the best decisions you can and you will be of the best service you can be to yourself and everyone around you. You will find peace. Whether you're retired and just want to lie on the beach or you're planning to still accomplish great things, you deserve to reap the benefits of your labor. You deserve to be happy even if your child isn't. It's okay to want to be happy.

Find a meeting. Build a support network. Surround yourself with people who move you forward in your life. Ask for what you need and be there for others in need. Your story has value to so many others. Share your experiences, your successes, and your missteps. People can learn what to do and what not to do. We shouldn't do this alone. There's no reason to do it alone. We need each other. We are all part of this one world, and it deserves us at our best.

ADDITIONAL RESOURCES

How To Survive Your Child's Addiction was not written to be a one-time read. It's a resource for you to refer to time and time again. It's a book that's meant to be shared and recommended to others who need it. Keep it on your nightstand or your desk. Get lost in the cover art. I had it designed to spark joy and wonder. Every time you look at it, you'll discover something new. I want this book to be an experience that elevates you from depths of chaos and crisis to the heights of peace and joy.

The tools offered in this book will only work if you take action. The changes have to come from you. I've created some valuable resources to help you that include guided meditations, videos and worksheets. You are not alone on this journey. I would love to connect with you and provide whatever support I can. Scan the QR code below to access all the support materials totally free of charge or visit my website at pattysfallone.com to learn more about my groups and coaching.

Quantity sales. Special discounts are available on quantity purchases by institutions, treatment facilities, municipalities and others. For details, please scan the QR code below or visit my website, pattysfallone.com

INDEX

Made in United States
Orlando, FL
22 November 2023

39289201R00124

#1 INTERNATIONAL BEST SELLING BOOK IN NINE CATEGORIES OF ADDICTION, RECOVERY & DRUG DEPENDENCY

Using relatable stories plus non-judgmental and no-nonsense language, How To Survive Your Child's Addiction provides practical tools that any parent can apply when coping with a child's addiction journey. A must-have support book.
— Donna S. Recovery Mom

An invaluable resource for any addiction professional to truly understand the unintended victims of addiction. — Mary Jonas, LMHC

Parenting a child with substance abuse issues is daunting. Through the confusion, shame, guilt, isolation and chaos, we begin to feel powerless as we allow our child's disease to rule our lives. When the parent is no longer in charge, the whole family spins out of control. In this tender but no-nonsense book, Ms. Fallone guides parents on a path of their own recovery. Parents learn better ways to navigate the challenges they face with their children, through simple and practical tools. They also learn how to restore peace in their own lives and are given permission to seek out joy. Through compassion and self-empowerment, parents learn the importance of practicing Soul Care, taking care of themselves and taking responsibility for how they are contributing to their own happiness. Parents learn how to step back into being in charge of their own lives, even if they are not in control.

Ms. Fallone is a Parent Recovery Coach in private practice who is dedicated to helping the underserved community of parents and loved ones of addicts through coaching, support groups and writing. After becoming frustrated by parents being told to focus on themselves and then only being given guides to help their children, she felt compelled to write a book that is truly focused on teaching parents what they need to do for themselves. She teaches parents how to nourish themselves so that they can find peace for themselves and show up better for all those they love.

ISBN 9781959840985
90000
9 781959 840985